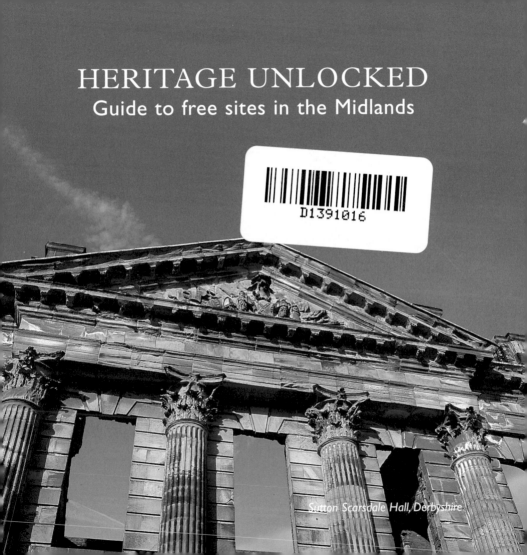

HERITAGE UNLOCKED
Guide to free sites in the Midlands

Sutton Scarsdale Hall, Derbyshire

CONTENTS

Among the many properties in the Midlands in the care of English Heritage are numerous sites where entry is free. This book, one of a series of regional guidebooks, provides a useful introduction to each of these free sites.

The great variety of these sites reflects the long history and diverse landscapes of the heart of England. The Peak District, for example, is the setting for some of this region's oldest and most enigmatic monuments, such as the curiously named Hob Hurst's House. The impressive remains of the Jewry Wall in Leicester attest to the region's importance during Roman occupation as a crossroads for major transport networks such as Watling Street and the Fosse Way.

Medieval castles and monastic ruins such as Clun Castle and White Ladies Priory, both in Shropshire, illustrate the wealth and power of leading families and the church in the Middle Ages. There are also smaller and more unusual monuments. These include the intricately carved stone cross at Geddington, Northamptonshire, erected in the late 13th century by Edward I to mark the stopping place of his wife Eleanor of Castile's funeral procession. In later centuries, the Midlands became renowned as the centre of the Industrial Revolution – among Britain's best-known industrial monuments is the world's first iron bridge, built over the River Severn in Shropshire in 1779.

Throughout the book, special features highlight aspects of the history and character of the Midlands. This guide aims to help visitors to discover, understand and enjoy some of the less well-known but nonetheless intriguing monuments in the care of English Heritage. A brief guide to English Heritage's admission-charging sites in the Midlands is also provided.

The church of St Mary and All Saints, Chesterfield, Derbyshire

WITHDRAWN

The East Midlands cover six counties: Derbyshire, Leicestershire, Lincolnshire, Northamptonshire, Nottinghamshire and Rutland, England's smallest. They encompass a wide variety of landscapes, from the hills and moorlands of the Peak District in the north to the lowlands, rich farmland and waterways in the east.

Among the earliest monuments are the henges, burial mounds and stone

circles found in Derbyshire. These include Arbor Low Henge and Stone Circle, which comprises a ring of more than 50 limestone slabs and fragments that now lie flat but once stood upright. This region also contains one of England's most important prehistoric archaeological sites, at Creswell Crags, on the border between Derbyshire and Nottinghamshire. Here, the first recorded examples of Ice Age cave art in the United Kingdom – engravings and relief carvings of animals – were identified in 2003.

The survival of Roman roads such as the Fosse Way, which extended from Devon to a new fortress at Lincoln, reveals the legacy of Roman occupation. In Lincoln, the route of the Fosse Way can be traced from the south of the city to the Roman arch at the North Gate. In Leicester, the Jewry Wall, 9m (30ft) high, is one of the largest sections of standing Roman masonry in Britain. A fragment of the Roman public baths, completed by the mid-second century AD, it has survived partly because it was later integrated into a Saxon church.

Left: Lincoln Cathedral, seen from Vicars' Court

Facing page: Mam Tor in the Peak District, Derbyshire

The power and riches of the bishops as princes of the church is reflected in the architecture of the Medieval Bishops' Palace, Lincoln, yet other ecclesiastical buildings can be found in more secluded locations. One example is Rufford Abbey in Nottinghamshire, completed in the late 12th century. In the second half of the 16th century, George Talbot, sixth Earl of Shrewsbury, converted the west range of the abbey into a house. The earl was the fourth and last husband of Bess of Hardwick, the richest and most powerful woman of the Elizabethan era after the queen herself. (Hardwick Old Hall, Derbyshire, was Bess's birthplace and family home.) Other monuments in the East Midlands are notable for their royal connections. Henry of Bolingbroke, who was crowned Henry IV after Richard II was deposed in 1399, was born at Bolingbroke Castle, Lincolnshire. The elegant stone cross at Geddington, Northamptonshire, was one of 12 built on the orders of Edward I to commemorate his wife, Eleanor of Castile, who died in 1290.

In this region historic wealth from farming is manifest in many surviving historic houses, and one of the most magnificent is Sutton Scarsdale Hall in Derbyshire. Although the building was reduced to a shell when it was sold after the First World War, its elegant Baroque stonework and fragments of finely detailed interior plasterwork can still be seen by visitors today.

The entrance hall of Sutton Scarsdale Hall, Derbyshire, as shown in Country Life, 1919

Arbor Low
Henge & Stone
Circle & Gib Hill
Barrow

Sutton
Scarsdale Hall

Mattersey
Priory

● *Gainsborough Old Hall*

*Peveril
Castle* ●

Hob Hurst's
House

● *Bolsover Castle*
Cundy House, Bolsover

● *Lincoln Medieval
Bishops' Palace*

Bolingbroke
Castle

● *Hardwick Old Hall*

Nine Ladies
Stone Circle

●

Rufford Abbey

Tattershall
College

*Wingfield
Manor*

● *Sibsey Trader
Windmill*

● *Ashby de la Zouch Castle*

*Kirby
Muxloe
Castle* ●

Jewry Wall

Lyddington Bede House ●

● *Kirby
Hall*

Eleanor Cross,
Geddington

●
*Rushton
Triangular
Lodge*

Chichele
College

Unstaffed sites
● *Staffed sites*

Arbor Low is a well-known and impressive prehistoric monument. Sometimes referred to as 'the Stonehenge of the North', owing to its henge bank and ditch, stone circle and cove, it bears more of a passing resemblance (though on a smaller scale) to that other great Neolithic monument, Avebury in Wiltshire.

The name Arbor Low appears to derive from 'Eorthburg Hlaw', meaning 'earthwork mound'. It consists of a massive bank and internal ditch surrounding a central area with stone settings. Today the bank stands to an average height of 2.1m (7ft), and its almost circular crest has a diameter of 79 x 75m (258 x 246ft). The substantial quarry ditch defines an oval central area with an approximate diameter of 40 x 52m (131 x 170ft). There are two gaps in the ditch and bank that form wide entrances to the north-west and south-south-east.

To the south-west, the henge bank has been disturbed by a large and later round barrow. Abutting the bank to the south-south-west are a low bank and ditch that run for some distance. The function and date of this linear bank are unknown, but it may be no more than an ancient field boundary built at a much later date than the henge.

Within the central area are the ruined and fallen remains – more than 50 large limestone slabs and fragments – of a large stone circle. When it was built it is likely that there were between 41 and 43 stones in the ring; these would have been set upright,

Arbor Low, one of the most impressive prehistoric monuments in the Peak District

most probably in shallow holes. At the centre of the monument are the remains of a group of stones known as the 'cove', which may originally have formed an upright rectangular box about 3–4m (10–13ft) wide.

Some 300m (328yd) south-west of the henge is the massive barrow known as Gib Hill. This is thought to be a Neolithic oval barrow with an Early Bronze Age round barrow superimposed at one end. This configuration can be seen by walking northwards downhill and looking back at the monument in profile. Excavations of the barrow by the Derbyshire antiquarian Thomas Bateman in the 19th century revealed human remains with a pottery vessel, as well as flint and other stone tools that appeared to be grave goods.

Arbor Low and Gib Hill form one of the most impressive complexes of prehistoric monuments in the Peak District. Nevertheless, there have been no excavations on either site for more than 100 years, and our understanding of their date, function and sequence of building is far from complete. By comparing them with better-studied sites elsewhere, however, it is possible that the Neolithic barrow at Gib Hill was the first element, perhaps followed by the bank and ditch of Arbor Low. The barrow over the henge ditch and the round barrow at Gib Hill are undoubtedly later features, as may be the stone circle and cove within the henge monument. It is important to remember that these monuments are the cumulative result of episodes of use that may have continued for more than 1,000 years, perhaps from about 2500 to 1500 BC.

All the earthworks are substantial and they would have taken a considerable time to build. Perhaps the co-operative acts of construction were as socially important as the monuments themselves. High on the false crest of a limestone ridge, Arbor Low would have been visible for many miles around – although the view of whatever took place inside it would have been restricted to those standing by the bank.

1/2 mile W of
A515, 2 miles S
of Monyash
OS Map 119,
ref SK 160636
Open 10am–6pm
daily in summer;
10am–4 pm daily
throughout rest
of year;
closed 24–26 Dec
and 1 Jan
Tel: 01629 816200
Farmer who owns
right of way to
the property may
levy a charge

CUNDY HOUSE, BOLSOVER

History

The Cundy House was built in the early 17th century to provide a water supply for Bolsover Castle, about 300m (328yd) away (see p. 95). The name 'Cundy' is a corruption of the French word 'conduit', or water pipe. Conduit houses were built for a number of country houses in this period. Usually unmanned and remote from the building they served, they had to be strong and secure, to protect the water supply from pollution by animals or from other interference. Four other smaller conduit houses were constructed about the same time along the ridge line on the far side of the castle.

The Cundy House, Bolsover

Built into the slope at the line of the natural spring, the structure housed a lead water tank. A water pipe from the Cundy House leads downwards to the main road and then up to the castle's cistern house, relying on the siphon effect to deliver water across the valley – a sophisticated use of technology. From the cistern house, water was pumped up to a higher level and then fed the early 17th-century Venus Fountain in the castle garden, which works today with an electric pump.

In 1885, the lead water tank was removed and taken to Welbeck Abbey, Nottinghamshire, and replaced by a brick-built tank. The Cundy House continued to supply water to the castle until the 1920s, when the pipe was cut during works on the main road in the valley. The Cundy House became a roofless ruin until its restoration in 2003.

Description

Despite its remote location and functional purpose, the Cundy House was carefully built. It is a rectangular structure with walls of neatly cut stone blocks. The path leads up a few steps to the single doorway, which has a projecting keystone, a feature found in Classical architecture. The little building is clearly intended to be viewed as a piece of architecture and not just as a functional structure. The original door would have been of thick oak boards and securely bolted. On the opposite gable there was a single window at high level, preventing unwanted access. It was probably sealed with iron bars but has since been blocked up.

The most extraordinary feature of the building is the roof, recently fully restored following careful research. It is formed not of timber and slates, but a solid stone vault, on top of which are thick roofing slabs, all rebuilt in the local magnesian limestone. Solid stone-vaulted roofs were often used on conduit houses, as they were secure and impervious to decay, unlike timber. The original coping stones at the gable ends were carefully cut to fit over the roof slabs, a vital clue for the recent restoration. Visible through the door grille are the closely fitting stones of the restored barrel-vaulted roof interior. In the centre of the building is the brick water tank, which still collects water.

Reconstruction drawing showing the water supply system from the Cundy House to Bolsover Castle

In Craggs Road, Bolsover, 6 miles E of Chesterfield on A362
OS Map 141, ref SK 470707
Tel: 01246 822844 (Bolsover Castle)

11

This site lies high on the gritstone moorlands of Harland Edge, above Beeley in the Peak District, reached from the nearest road by a stiff uphill walk of about 2km (1¼ miles). The word 'hob' – meaning a sprite, bogey or hobgoblin – features in many Peak District place names. This place may have been known locally as belonging to 'Hob o' th' Hurst'.

The monument comprises a rectangular mound measuring 8 x 7.5m (26 x 25ft) retained by drystone walling. Surrounding the mound are a steep-sided ditch and low outer bank, which at its crest measures 16 x 16.5m (52 x 54ft). The ditch may be a later feature, from a time when stone was taken from the site to build nearby drystone walls. On the north side the bank has been damaged by a packhorse track.

At the centre of the mound is a rectangular cluster of stones, measuring 3.5 x 2m (11½ x 6½ ft) internally. Although the stones might have functioned as a burial chamber, with the spaces between them

spanned by capstones, they might also have been designed as an open setting. Thomas Bateman excavated the site in 1853 and found evidence of a cremation, and two pieces of galena, or lead ore, surrounded by an arc of small stones.

Many of the barrow mounds in the Peak District are known to date from the Bronze Age, although the unusual form of this example has led some to suggest that it might be significantly later, perhaps of Iron Age date.

Facing page: Aerial view of Hob Hurst's House, high in the moorlands of the Peak District

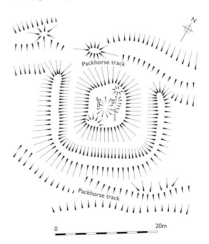

Plan of Hob Hurst's House

Off unclassified road off B5057, 9 miles W of Chesterfield

OS Map 119, ref SK 287692

Tel: 01629 816200

13

CRESWELL CRAGS

Straddling the border between Nottinghamshire and Derbyshire, and close to both Worksop and Bolsover, Creswell Crags is one of England's most important archaeological and geological sites. Here there are 23 caves, flanking the sides of a spectacular gorge naturally formed from magnesian limestone. As one of the most northerly places on earth to have been visited by humans during the last Ice Age, the site is of international scientific significance.

The fossil record of animal bones found in the caves extends back about 125,000 years. Neanderthal populations used the caves about 50,000 years ago and modern humans about 20,000 years later. When the earth's climate began to warm up about 13,000 years ago, after the coldest phase of the Ice Age, the caves were once again inhabited. Human use and occupation of the caves continued sporadically well into recorded history.

The earliest known portable art in the United Kingdom – figures engraved onto animal bones – was found at Creswell Crags and, in 2003, the UK's first recorded examples of Ice Age cave art were identified on the wall of Church Hole Cave. Some 12 carvings have been identified in the cave, including depictions of reindeer, bison, birds and geometric shapes. A programme of scientific dating has confirmed that they are at least 12,800 years old.

Creswell Crags Gorge from the air

More than 750,000 animal bones have been found in the caves, as well as more than 4,000 stone tools and waste from their manufacture and resharpening. Study of this important archaeological resource has revealed much about the development and adaptation of animals and people during a period of profound climatic change. It has also provided a great deal of information about species that are extinct or that no longer survive in the United Kingdom, for example mammoth, woolly rhinoceros, hyena and bear.

Archaeological interest in Creswell Crags began in the 1860s, and there have been many excavations since then. In recent years, Creswell Heritage Trust, which manages the site, has worked to improve the record and accessibility of the cave finds. There have also been major environmental improvements, which include the removal of the sewage works, and plans are well advanced to replace the Crags Road, which runs through the gorge, with a bridleway. A museum and education centre, with a display about the cave art, are located at the east end of the gorge. Tours to Robin Hood Cave and Church Hole Cave to see the cave art run regularly from the museum (for more information, visit www.creswell-crags.org.uk).

Above: This Ice Age carving of a deer was one of the recent discoveries in the caves

Below: Ice Age rock engravings of birds were also found in the caves

Stanton Moor is situated on elevated ground to the west of the River Derwent, near Bakewell in the Peak District. Few of the thousands of visitors who enjoy the tranquillity of the moor and the fine views can fail to notice the widespread archaeological remains that are dotted across this landscape. Most of these are thought to date from the Bronze Age, about 3,000 to 4,000 years ago. More than 70 stone cairns and barrows are known, and excavations over the past 100 years have demonstrated that many served as places of burial. The most evocative and well-known of

Nine Ladies Stone Circle. Despite the name, there are actually 10 stones in the circle

Facing page: *The circle may have served as a meeting place, landmark, or place of ceremony or burial*

these monuments is the Nine Ladies Stone Circle and the King Stone, set 40m (131ft) to the west-south-west of the circle.

Despite the name, there are 10 stones within the circle, the tenth (which has fallen and now lies flat) having been located in 1977. The stones are set on the inner edge of a slight bank, and form a ring which measures 11.5 x 10.5m (38 x 34ft). The monument was first recorded by Major Hayman Rooke in 1782. He noted that there appeared to be stones in the centre of the ring, which may have formed a small cairn or 'cist'.

The names of the monuments derive from their associations with folk traditions, in which it is said that nine women were dancing on the Sabbath to a fiddler – the King Stone – and were turned to stone. The graffiti carved on the King Stone, which includes the name 'Bill Stumps', is also mentioned in *The Pickwick Papers* by Charles Dickens.

In common with many other stone circles, little evidence has been uncovered to suggest why or when this stone circle was built and how it was used. Suggestions include a place for ceremony or burial, a territorial marker, a perceived link between the earth and the sky and the living and the dead, or a meeting place for seasonal events. Such monuments may have had many functions, their uses and perceived significance shifting over time.

Off unclassified road off A6, 5 miles SE of Bakewell OS Map 119, ref SK 249635 Tel: 01629 816200

SUTTON SCARSDALE HALL

History

Sutton Scarsdale Hall was built in the Baroque style on the site of an existing house between 1724 and 1729 for the fourth Earl of Scarsdale. The architect for the new hall was Francis Smith of Warwick, who skilfully incorporated the earlier building of about 1469 within his design. Notable craftsmen were employed here: Edward Poynton of Nottingham carved the exterior stonework and the Italian master craftsmen Arturi and Vasalli carried out the fine stucco (plasterwork) detailing in the principal rooms, remnants of which can still be seen. Grinling Gibbons is believed to have contributed some of the interior wood carvings. The cost of this splendid building left the Scarsdale heirs with depleted funds and they were eventually forced to sell the hall in the 19th century.

John Arkwright, a descendant of the industrialist Richard Arkwright (see p. 20), bought the hall, but in 1919 the family sold it to a company of asset strippers. Many of its finely decorated rooms were sold off as architectural salvage and the house was reduced to a shell. Some rooms still exist: three interiors are displayed at the Museum of Art in Philadelphia. A pine-panelled room is at the Huntington Library, California. It was offered to the Huntington by a Hollywood film producer who had used it as a set for a film, *Kitty*, in 1934. He had bought it from William Randolph Hearst, the newspaper magnate and well-known collector.

The eastern front of Sutton Scarsdale Hall, built in the Baroque style in 1724–9

The ruins of the hall were saved from demolition by the writer Sir Osbert Sitwell, who bought it in 1946 after he had heard of the impending sale to dismantle the stonework. In 1970 descendants of the Sitwells persuaded the Department of the Environment to take the building into guardianship and preserve it for the nation. A recent programme of works has been undertaken by English Heritage to preserve and protect the fragments of the original stucco interior.

Description

The ruins of Sutton Scarsdale Hall, with tantalising remnants of a once majestic interior, offer the visitor an opportunity to view the 'skeleton' of the building – impossible in more complete country houses. The approach to the hall today is along a narrow driveway. Its spectacular location on a hillside is immediately apparent. The roofless hall is built of mellow sandstone and stands to its original parapet height. Some areas of stonework have been lost at this level, giving an almost castellated appearance from a distance. The medieval church of St Mary stands to the right. On entering the site, the visitor faces the rear (west elevation) of the building. There are two projections denoting the U-shaped plan of the hall; that to the right housed the kitchen and service areas.

The hall was built with two impressive facades. The eastern front is the grandest, with exuberant Baroque detail typified by attached giant Corinthian columns topped with a central pediment. The central bays housed the formal drawing room. Elements of the 15th-century structure such as blocked window openings in earlier brickwork can be seen in this room and in the one behind it.

The slightly plainer north elevation housed the entrance hall (see p. 6), which contains remnants of stucco work. The remains of the paired Ionic pilasters with wreathed swags are clearly visible, as are the remains of the chimney pieces incorporating carved figures.

Between
Chesterfield
and Bolsover,
1½ miles S of
Arkwright Town
OS Map 120,
ref SK 442689
Open 10am–6pm
daily in summer;
10am–4pm daily
throughout rest
of year;
closed 24–26
Dec and 1 Jan

Technological innovation in the valley of the River Derwent in Derbyshire changed the world. The famous series of 18th-century water-powered textile mills, over a 15-mile stretch of the valley from Derby towards Cromford and Matlock Bath, is renowned internationally as the 'cradle of the new factory system'. This early industrial landscape was inscribed on the World Heritage List in December 2001 in recognition of its 'outstanding universal value'.

Lombe's Mill in Derby, built by Sir Thomas and John Lombe in 1721, was the first in England to employ technology that had been developed in Italy and that enabled silk to be thrown on machines driven by water power. It was Sir Richard Arkwright's Cromford Mill, built in 1771, however, that provided the true blueprint for factory production. Arkwright had designed a spinning frame on which raw cotton could be spun into thread, for which he had taken out a patent in 1769. Arkwright's activities stimulated collaboration with other

Portrait of Sir Richard Arkwright by Joseph Wright of Derby (1790)

entrepreneurs such as Jedediah Strutt, Thomas Evans and Peter Nightingale.

The surviving mills at Darley Abbey and Belper incorporate technological innovations such as fireproof construction. Weirs and watercourses harnessed the energy of the River Derwent to power the early textile machinery. The landscape of the Derwent Valley also bears the imprint of the transport systems, farms, ancillary industries and social and economic infrastructure of thriving industrial communities in the late 18th and 19th centuries. Moreover, the history and character of the area continue to underpin a healthy sense of identity for the communities that live and work in the Derwent Valley today.

The Derwent Valley Mills World Heritage Site is accessible on foot from the Derwent Valley Heritage Way and by train from stations along the former North Midland Railway line between Derby and Matlock.

The former turnpike road (the A6) criss-crosses the River Derwent, linking the mill settlements at Darley Abbey, Milford, Belper and Cromford. Masson Mill and Cromford lie at the northern end of the valley, and Derby's former Silk Mill is the first stop for visitors coming from the south. The Derwent Valley Visitor Centre in North Mill, Belper, celebrates the area's textile traditions.

Cromford

Richard Arkwright's first mill, dating from 1771, is being carefully repaired and restored by the Arkwright Society, the local civic society in the Matlock area. This major project rescued Cromford Mill from threatened demolition in 1979. At Cromford, Arkwright extended the scale and range of mechanised cotton production, and introduced a management system founded on the division of labour, which contributed to his success as an entrepreneur.

A second mill at Cromford was constructed in 1776–7, financed by Peter Nightingale, a lead merchant and landowner. Technological innovation appeared in the form of a primitive convector heating system installed in 1789. Nearby Cromford Wharf marks the end of the Cromford Canal, built in the 1790s as part of a through route to Manchester. The highways, byways and watercourses of Cromford village thread their way between some of the earliest surviving millworkers' housing, dating from 1776 onwards.

Arkwright's Cotton Mills by Night *(about 1782–3)* *by Joseph Wright of Derby*

THE DERWENT VALLEY MILLS

Masson Mill

The fine architectural detail of Sir Richard Arkwright's Masson Mill, built in 1783, contrasts with the characteristic red-brick extensions built by the English Sewing Cotton Company in 1911 and 1928. The prominent mill chimney and engine house were built by Stott & Sons in 1900.

Belper

Jedediah Strutt built his first mill here in 1776–7, and a second was erected in 1784. Belper's massive red-brick East Mill, built by the English Sewing Cotton Company in 1912, dominates the northern end of the town. In its shadow is the important early iron-framed North Mill (1805), which overlooks the famous horseshoe weir. The North Mill is a small fragment of the former Strutt mills that were demolished in the 1960s. Constructed in iron and brick, and with plaster cladding, it was among the first mills to be fireproof. Millworkers' housing lines the regular streets laid out by the Strutt Estate on land to the south of Belper Mills.

Milford

The late 19th-century chimney of the dyehouse marks the site of the former Milford Mills built by Strutt from about 1784 onwards. Sinuous terraces of millworkers' housing line the steep sides of the valley overlooking the Hopping Mill Weir where the waters of the River Derwent powered the textile machinery.

Masson Mill, further up the valley from Cromford, built by Arkwright in 1783

Darley Abbey

The Boars Head Mill complex built by the Evans brothers at Darley Abbey is among the most complete of any of the early cotton factory sites. The Long Mill (1782–9) has a primitive form of fire protection: the exposed wooden structural members are covered with metal sheaths. The West and East Mills of 1819–21 have brick floors and cast-iron columns. The millworkers' housing at Darley Abbey includes some of the interesting 'clusters' (four houses built back-to-back) also adopted by the Strutt Estate in Belper.

Above: The Boars Head Mills at Darley Abbey, built in the late 18th and early 19th centuries

Right: The former Derby Silk Mill, now the Industrial Museum

Derby

Massive stone arches over the watercourses of the River Derwent are all that survive of the original Lombe's Mill, destroyed by fire in 1910. It was rebuilt three storeys high, and the south-west stair tower incorporates the brickwork of the original building. It was later converted to house Derby Industrial Museum. Derby Museum and Art Gallery also contains a fine series of portraits and paintings depicting the Derwent Valley Mills and their famous owners.

The conduit for the Roman baths at Leicester, completed in the mid-second century AD

History

Before the Roman conquest there was a settlement on the eastern bank of the River Soar, centred on the area of St Nicholas Circle in the heart of modern Leicester. This was Ratae ('the ramparts'), a major centre of the Corieltauvi tribe, whose territory stretched from Birmingham to the Lincolnshire coast. In the first century AD, a Roman fort was probably established here, where the Fosse Way – the new road from Devon to the fortress at Lincoln – crossed the Soar.

A grid of streets was laid out for the Roman town in an area now bounded by the river, Sanvey Gate, Church Gate and Horsefair Street. In the second century, the town's public buildings included the forum (the administrative centre and market) sited between Cross Street, a major Roman thoroughfare, and Holy Bones; and the public baths, which were completed by AD 160. The Jewry Wall is a fragment of these baths. It has survived partly because it was later incorporated into the Saxon church of St Nicholas. This utilised one of the Roman arches for the west door of its porch, which no longer exists.

Description

The Jewry Wall is one of the most massive survivals of Roman masonry in Britain. It is built from several types of rubble, particularly granite and slate from Charnwood Forest, and local sandstones; narrow Roman bricks have been used extensively to level the rough material. The large blocks at Roman ground level are of millstone grit from near Melbourne in Derbyshire. The small holes in the wall (later plugged) mark the position of the wooden scaffolding used during construction.

On the east side, beside the church of St Nicholas, the wall has a series of brick arches, two of which are pierced by doorways; a smaller arch was probably a niche for a statue. This was the west side of a large exercise hall (*palaestra*), on the site of the present churchyard. From this hall the bather walked through one of the arched doors into a rectangular, unheated room (*frigidarium*), on either side of which were three smaller spaces: latrines and changing rooms. Beyond were three warm rooms (*tepidaria*) with underfloor heating (hypocausts), and then three much larger halls (*caldaria*) which were heated to a high temperature. Here the bather could relax and sweat out the grime of the day, taking a dip in one of the three hot plunge pools set into the far walls. On the north and south sides were two other baths

of cooler water. (The foundations of the hot plunge pools and of the three furnaces that provided the heat lie beneath the modern building, designed by Trevor Dannatt in 1962.)

On the south side, towards St Nicholas Circle, is the massive conduit, its single roofing slab indicating Roman ground level here. Water for the Roman town was brought in by an aqueduct, the course of which is marked by the west side of Aylestone Road and Oxford Street. A portion survives at the junction with Saffron Lane.

Below: The section of the Roman wall beside St Nicholas's Church

In St Nicholas Circle, W of church of St Nicholas
OS Map 140, ref SK 582045
Open: 10am–6pm daily in summer; 10am–4pm daily throughout rest of year; museum open Sat only 11am–4.30pm; closed 24–26 Dec and 1 Jan
Tel: 0116 225 4971 (Jewry Wall Museum)

FROM THE ROMANS TO THE SPACE AGE

Leicester's architectural tradition runs uninterrupted from Roman times to the present day. Notable buildings in the city include the Roman remains at Jewry Wall (see pp. 24–5); England's only surviving pedestrian promenade, the tree-lined New Walk of 1785; and the National Space Centre (2001) at Abbey Meadows, designed by Nicholas Grimshaw and Partners.

Settlement at Leicester pre-dates the Roman occupation of Britain: there was a well-established community on the River Soar's east bank during the Iron Age. By AD 100 this settlement had become the Roman administrative centre of the Celtic tribe of the Corieltauvi. By the mid-second century, the forum and bath complex, now known as the Jewry Wall, were being built. The town defences, established in the early third century AD and later rebuilt in stone, survived until the late 18th century, but the Roman and medieval street patterns are still evident in Highcross Street, Southgates and High Street (formerly Swines Market).

By the 680s, a bishopric of Leicester had been founded, and by the late ninth century

Leicester Cathedral from New Street, in 1957

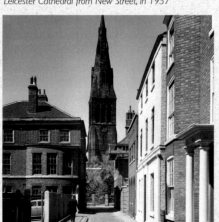

The War Memorial by Edwin Lutyens in Victoria Park

the town had become one of the main centres of the Danelaw, the Danish-ruled area of Britain. Saxon building work can still be seen, especially in St Nicholas's Church, next to Jewry Wall. Leicester's medieval prosperity is reflected in its surviving architecture of the Middle Ages. In Castle Yard, the Great Hall, built by Robert 'le Bossu' between 1152 and 1168, is thought to contain the earliest timber roof of a residential building in Europe. In the neighbouring church of St Mary de Castro, originally founded in 1107 by le Bossu's father, the first Earl of Leicester, the county's finest Norman decoration can be found in the chancel sedilia (seats for those celebrating mass).

Worsted thread was key to Leicester's late medieval prosperity, and the advent of framework knitting in 1680 and powered spinning mills in the mid-19th century expanded the industry further. By the 1880s, Leicester's renown was founded on its hosiery and

shoe industries, the towering mill and factory buildings of which still stand. But these remain only relics, as Leicester's traditional industries declined dramatically in the last quarter of the 20th century.

Much fine architecture survives from the 18th century onwards, from the Georgian buildings clustered around the cathedral to the Victorian banks, churches and other civic architecture, reflecting Leicester's late 19th-century boom. Arts and Crafts suburbs lead to the south, while the 20th century is well represented in Victoria Park's War Memorial by Edwin Lutyens and the University of Leicester's Engineering Building (1959) by Stirling & Gowan. Today Leicester can boast a richly diverse society which has created new architectural expressions of faith and culture, such as the Jain Centre, and Belgrave Gate's 'Golden Mile', with its many Asian restaurants.

The National Space Centre by Nicholas Grimshaw and Partners

BOLINGBROKE CASTLE

Facing page: Plan of Bolingbroke Castle

Henry of Bolingbroke, later Henry IV, depicted in a 15th-century manuscript

History

Bolingbroke Castle was one of three castles built by Ranulf de Blundeville, Earl of Chester and Lincoln, in the 1220s after his return from the Crusades (the others being Beeston Castle, Cheshire, and Chartley, Staffordshire). After Blundeville's death, the castle remained in the ownership of the Earls of Lincoln and was later inherited through marriage by John of Gaunt, Duke of Lancaster. An extremely powerful member of the royal court, John of Gaunt became the guardian of Richard II when the young king succeeded to the throne at the age of 10.

John of Gaunt and his first wife, Blanche, lived at the castle during the 1360s; their son, Henry of Bolingbroke, was born there in 1366. Henry had a tempestuous relationship with Richard II and was exiled in 1397. He returned to England after the death of his father in 1399, enraged that the king had seized the estates he had inherited. Richard was in Ireland, attempting to quell a rising, when he heard of Henry's return.

These events marked the end of Richard II's reign. Henry of Bolingbroke was encouraged to claim the throne of England from his unpopular rival, and Richard was imprisoned. Soon afterwards, Henry was crowned king as Henry IV. There is no documentary evidence to suggest that Henry IV ever returned to his birthplace.

The main function of the castle during the 15th and 16th centuries was as an administrative centre for the estates of the Duchy of Lancaster. The current names of the towers, for example the Auditor's Tower and Receiver's Tower, refer to their use during this period.

Surveys undertaken at the castle in the 17th century show that only a few of the towers then remained in use and that the enclosing walls were extremely dilapidated. During the Civil War (1642–8), the castle became a defensible base for a Royalist garrison and was besieged by Parliamentarian forces in 1643. The Royalists surrendered that winter, and the entire castle was destroyed. Bolingbroke has remained a ruin for more than 350 years.

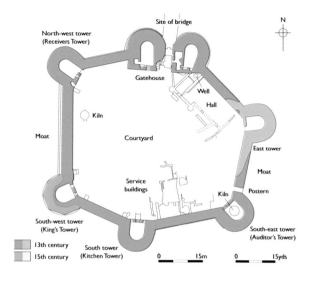

Description

The visitor enters through the gatehouse towers into the open central area of the castle. Bolingbroke Castle is a prime example of 13th-century architectural design and is described as an 'enclosure' castle. Such castles are characterised by curtain walls with towers enclosing a courtyard. Within this courtyard there would have been timber-framed structures, including a great hall and service buildings, evidence of which was found in excavations during the 1960s.

The south-west tower, which is now known as the King's Tower, was rebuilt between 1444 and 1456 on an octagonal plan. By this time, the castle was more than 200 years old, and this remodelling represents an attempt by the owners to express their wealth and importance.

From the Auditor's Tower can be seen the Rout Yard – the field to the south of the castle – which contains several earthworks, including a rectangular enclosure. Debate continues as to the original use of this earthwork, which may have been a fishpond, an animal compound or a 17th-century fort.

In Old Bolingbroke, 16 miles N of Boston off A16
OS Map 122, ref TF 349650
Tel: 01529 461499
(Heritage Trust of Lincolnshire)

The village of Tattershall is dominated by the 15th-century castle, bought and restored by Lord Curzon of Kedleston in the early 20th century. Its great tower, one of the earliest and most impressive brick buildings in the county, is now in the care of the National Trust.

The castle and estate were inherited by Ralph, Lord Cromwell, in 1417. He became Henry VI's treasurer and his marriage to the heiress Margaret Deincourt brought him further lands and wealth.

The interior of Tattershall College

Between 1434 and his death in 1456, he embarked upon a great programme of building in Tattershall. He extended the castle with the impressive great tower, added a number of smaller brick buildings within the walls and excavated an outer moat.

His building projects in the village were not confined to his own domestic comforts. In 1440, while work continued on the castle, Lord Cromwell issued a charter creating a college of secular canons who would serve the church and act as chantry priests to pray for his soul. This was an age in which lay men and women would leave money and lands to monasteries, churches and colleges to ensure prayers were said for their souls after their deaths. Cromwell was an extremely rich man with no direct heirs and so could afford to make elaborate arrangements.

Tattershall College was built in 1460, four years after the death of its patron, Lord Cromwell, and was completed by William of Wainfleet, Bishop of Winchester. This building formed part of the complex of college buildings in Tattershall village and is thought to have been the grammar school. Most colleges provided such educational facilities for their choristers and for the sons of local tenants. Schoolmasters from the clergy and the laity might teach in both the collegiate and secular schools.

The Chantries Act of 1547 led to the closure of this type of religious institution across the country, and the college buildings near the church at Tattershall were demolished. The present building was refounded as a secular grammar school and continued to be used for this purpose until the late 17th century. The new tenant converted the buildings into a malt-house and granary. Many further alterations were made to the building until it came into state guardianship in 1972.

Description

The college is built in red brick with limestone ashlar dressings. The original structure would have been two

One of the Tudor arched doorways

storeys high, but later a cellar was inserted. This has now been filled in, and the ground floor is set halfway between the level of the original floor and the cellar floor. Original openings such as the Tudor arched doorways remain, and their positions in the long walls indicate the original floors of the 15th-century building.

The college, having retained much of its original fabric, is now one of the oldest brick structures in England. What remains is an almost complete example of the Perpendicular style of architecture.

In Tattershall,
14 miles NE of
Sleaford on A153
*OS Map 122;
ref TF 213578*
Tel: 01529 461499
(Heritage Trust of
Lincolnshire)

Lincoln's heritage is the centrepiece of the city's regeneration programme. The Medieval Bishops' Palace, in the guardianship of English Heritage, is an exemplar of best practice in the display of a major ruin: it has an award-winning visitor centre and a Contemporary Heritage Garden, where the best of modern design enhances the remains of the past, and where new conservation techniques can be tested. The city has several brownfield sites, many of which are scheduled ancient monuments and all of which are archaeologically sensitive. With careful planning and

Above: Lincoln Cathedral and the Medieval Bishops' Palace
Right: Castle Square, Lincoln

informed advice on the least damaging methods of construction, these are now being sympathetically redeveloped. An area that was once a poorly designed car park is the site of a major new museum for the city and county that opened in April 2005.

The sound understanding of Lincoln's buried archaeology that makes such regeneration projects possible is based on many years of rescue excavation, the use of a pioneering Urban Archaeology Database that informs all planning decisions, and the Lincoln Archaeological Research Assessment which directs future research. All of these were supported by English Heritage from their inception. English Heritage's archaeological survey team has

analysed the earthworks of the West and South Commons as the first part of a national survey, and a two-year programme that will further our understanding of the development and significance of the Lincoln townscape is being trialled. In both cases, there is strong community involvement. Yet despite the city's cultural richness, Lincoln also contains some of the poorest areas in the country. A partnership grant scheme has levered in substantial private investment to regenerate business premises and community facilities in Monks Road and the lower High Street, by repairing and restoring historic buildings which had been in long-term decline.

The greatest improvement to the historic city will be the removal of heavy through traffic, and English Heritage has been working in partnership with Lincolnshire County Council to determine the best route for an eastern bypass. The road proposed would run across the Witham Valley, one of the most important wetlands in Europe. Here, there have been significant finds of prehistoric and later metalwork since the late 18th century. In conjunction with the Environment Agency, which is undertaking a massive flood defence scheme, English Heritage facilitated the excavation of an Iron Age timber causeway at Fiskerton, the finds from which form one of the major displays in the new city museum. Research on re-watering in the valley has been undertaken with local landowners, and a major archaeological survey of the Fiskerton area has been carried out. The valley has the highest concentration of medieval monasteries in Britain. These are being recorded as part of the Lincolnshire Limewoods Project, which will promote public access to the natural and historic environment of Lincoln's hinterland.

The Contemporary Heritage Garden in the Medieval Bishops' Palace

CHICHELE COLLEGE

History

Chichele College was founded by Henry Chichele, Archbishop of Canterbury from 1414 to 1443 and the founder of All Souls' College, Oxford. He was born in Higham Ferrers in about 1362. The buildings here were partly complete when the foundation ceremony took place in 1425.

The term 'college' was then used to describe a community of priests who shared a communal life that was less strictly controlled than that within a monastery. Chichele is a rare surviving example of a chantry college, a type of institution common in England in the 14th and 15th centuries. The colleges' prime concern was to offer prayers for the souls of the patron and his family, and often they also had an educational function. Chichele College was provided with a master, seven chaplains, four clerks and six choristers. It had close links with the parish church, and the town's school and bedehouse (almshouse), for the 'deserving' poor and elderly.

The college was surrendered to Henry VIII in 1542, and the building has been much altered since, so that many of the original features have disappeared. Parts of the south and east ranges were adapted to form a smaller building, which in the 18th century served as an inn. By the early 20th century it was reduced to a single farm cottage with an attached granary.

Description

Although parts of the college survive only as foundations, some impressive walls remain and the chapel is still

Chichele College, viewed from the north-east

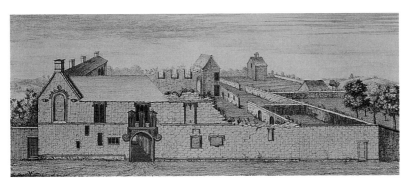

An 18th-century engraving of Chichele College by Samuel and Nathaniel Buck

In Higham Ferrers, on A6 OS Map 153, ref SP 960687 For access to the chapel, please contact the keykeeper, Mrs D. Holyoak, 12 Lancaster St, Higham Ferrers. Tel: 01933 314157. For full details of current displays visit www.east-northamptonshire.gov.uk Tel: 01933 655401

roofed. The buildings were laid out around a quadrangle about 14m (45ft) square. The east wall of the east range, which fronts the main road, stands to its full height and incorporates the main entrance gateway. At its north end another wall abutting it, with a blocked opening, is the remnant of a barn built in the late 18th or early 19th century that overlies parts of the north and east ranges.

Much of the south range, which includes the accommodation block and chapel, survives. The chapel has been much altered and partly rebuilt, but retains a large, blocked east window. Built into both its interior and exterior walls are projecting corbels, carved in the form of human heads, probably placed here after the college was suppressed. The chapel is now regularly used for art exhibitions.

To the north and west of the present building are exposed foundations and stone walls. These include the remains of the western part of the south range and other buildings. The foundations suggest that a hall took up all or most of the west range, with the kitchens at the north-west corner. The level, grassed area on the western edge of the site represents the college garden, laid out in 1425.

*The Eleanor Cross
at Geddington*

History

When Eleanor of Castile, the first wife
of Edward I, died at Harby, near
Lincoln, in 1290, the grief-stricken king
was driven to create the most elaborate
series of funerary monuments to any
queen of England. He ordered the
building of 12 elegant crosses to
mark each of the resting places of his
wife's funeral procession as it travelled
from Lincoln to her burial place at
Westminster Abbey, London. The best-
preserved of these lies at the centre of
the little village of Geddington.

Edward had married Eleanor,
daughter of Ferdinand III of Castile,
in 1254. Their marriage was politically
unpopular, yet notably successful in
personal terms, and the couple had
16 children. They were rarely apart,
and Eleanor even travelled with
Edward on Crusade to the Holy
Land. At her death, aged 47, on
28 November 1290, she had been
accompanying Edward on his way
north to fight the Scots.

The cross at Geddington was
erected opposite St Mary Magdalene

Church, where the cortège had rested on the night of 6 December 1290, next to a royal hunting lodge. Until the Reformation, prayers were said at all the crosses on the anniversary of Queen Eleanor's death; a mass is still said annually for her at Geddington.

Of the original 12 crosses only two others remain: one at Hardingstone, near Northampton, and another – heavily restored – in Waltham Cross, Hertfordshire. A replica cross was built on the site of a lost original at Charing Cross, London, in 1863. Queen Eleanor's gilded bronze effigy can still be seen in Westminster Abbey.

Detail of the gilt-bronze effigy of Eleanor of Castile in Westminster Abbey, London

Description

The Geddington cross is different from the typical stone crosses that once stood in nearly every city, town and village in England. These took various forms and served many social and religious functions. Many were destroyed during or after the Reformation. Spire-shaped crosses, of which the Eleanor Crosses are the most famous, are unusual.

With its subtle geometry and rich decoration, the Eleanor Cross is an outstanding example of late 13th-century stone carving. It was built in the new, highly ornamental English Decorated style, using local limestone. Intricately carved with floral patterns, the slender cross is triangular in plan and stands nearly 12.8m (42ft) tall. It is built in three tiers. Below the tapering pinnacle at the top are three canopied niches, each containing a Caen stone figure of Eleanor. Beneath these figures are six shields, two on each face, bearing the arms of Castile, Leon, England, and Ponthieu in France, of which Eleanor was countess. Originally, the pinnacle would have been crowned by a cross.

In the centre of Geddington, off A43 between Kettering and Corby; car park off Queen Street OS Map 141, ref SP 894830

THE BOOT AND SHOE INDUSTRY

Visitors to Northamptonshire may be surprised to discover that many of the county's towns and villages were global centres of boot- and shoe-making during much of the 19th and 20th centuries. Indeed, some historic factories, such as Church's, Grenson's and Crockett & Jones, still produce high-quality men's shoes for an international market. The industry has contracted in recent decades, yet many Northamptonshire neighbourhoods still derive their identity and character from the good, solid, functional brick buildings which were erected in the late 19th and early 20th centuries to serve the industry.

Northampton was already an important centre of boot- and shoe-making in the 17th century, when the town supplied boots for Oliver Cromwell's troops in Ireland. But it was only from the mid-19th century – as mechanisation began to take over – that the industry made a visible impact on the built environment. Northampton greatly expanded, as did other towns such as Kettering, Raunds, Rushden, Wellingborough, and villages such as Long Buckby. In Kettering, in particular, one can still see hundreds of small garden workshops where shoemakers worked by themselves, undertaking manual tasks such as riveting and closing (sewing uppers). In Long Buckby, a group of late 19th-century workshops lies behind a short terrace of houses, occupying the first floors of outbuildings which also contain water closets and coal sheds. Near to workers' houses were the factories where mechanised processes were carried out. This unusual combination of outworking and factory production endured well into the 20th century.

Above: Dickens Brothers Leather Works, Northampton, in about 1929

Left: The former Church's factory, Duke Street, Northampton

In the streets of Northamptonshire towns, boot and shoe factories can be identified by their characteristic metal-framed windows, loading doors and winches, and sometimes by ornamental stone plaques and date stones – fortunately, these features are often retained when buildings are converted to new uses. Examples include the former Church's factory, Duke Street, Northampton, which was the company's main manufacturing site from 1877 until the 1950s. After the factory closed in the 1990s, the large extension of 1893 was converted into apartments. The Crockett & Jones factory in Perry Street, Northampton, built in five phases between the 1880s and 1930s. It is surrounded by terraced housing which

would have been occupied by many boot and shoe workers. Burkitt & Son's small upper and legging factory is tucked between terraced houses on Victoria Road, Wellingborough. Despite its size, the building displayed considerable architectural pretension and clearly served as an advertisement for the company.

A representative selection of the machinery which once filled the boot and shoe factories can be seen in the Northampton Central Museum and Art Gallery on Guildhall Road. A walking tour of the main boot- and shoe-making district of Northampton, and more information about the buildings of the industry, can be found in *Built to Last? The Buildings of the Northamptonshire Boot and Shoe Industry* (English Heritage, 2004).

Above: *Burkitt & Son's factory, Wellingborough*

Left: *Late 19th-century shoe-making workshops in Long Buckby*

MATTERSEY PRIORY

The priory of St Helen stands on a gravel island on the west side of the River Idle, in what was marshland in the Middle Ages. It was established in 1185 by Roger fitzRalph of nearby Mattersey for the Gilbertine Order, the only monastic order to have originated in England. St Gilbert founded the order at Sempringham, Lincolnshire, between 1131 and 1148, originally for women, but with lay sisters and brothers and canons to serve the spiritual needs of the community. There were 26 Gilbertine monasteries, but only 11 housed both nuns and canons. Mattersey was a house of canons only, and its layout is similar to that of monasteries of the Augustinian Order, whose modified rule the canons adopted.

The remains date mainly from the late 13th century – the original monastery was destroyed by fire in 1279. The badly ruined church, on the north side of the cloister, is of an earlier date. It was rectangular in plan, with the choir of the canons towards its east end, and that for the lay brothers to the west. In the 15th century, a tower was built overlying the north wall of the church, which may have been partly ruinous, as lay brothers were no longer a significant part of the community by that date. The monastery was suppressed in 1538 when the whole of the order was surrendered to the Crown.

The canons lived in the east range of the cloister, built immediately after the fire of 1279. The ground floor comprised a vaulted space of seven bays. The northern two bays were chapels, originally entered from the

The refectory at Mattersey Priory

church: the canons said personal masses daily. The next three bays comprised the chapter house where the community met to discuss business and to receive discipline. The two bays at the southern end, separated from the chapter house by a timber partition, formed part of a cross-wing extending to the east. This was the day room where the canons could work within the cloister, and it may also have been the warming house where a fire was kept during winter and spring. To the east of this is the paved drain of the first-floor communal latrine that served the dormitory on the upper floor.

The south range housed the canons' refectory above a vaulted ground floor. Although also late 13th-century, it is slightly later than the east range. The use of the upper floor for dining was an intentional reference to the Last Supper and was the norm in canons' houses. At the south-west corner of the range are the low walls of a kitchen.

The west range, built in the first half of the 14th century, was the lay brothers' range, with their refectory on the ground floor and dormitory above. Between this range and the church was the outer parlour, where the community could meet outsiders. When lay brothers ceased to be a significant part of the community in the late 14th century, the west range was almost certainly converted into a house for the prior. The cloister was surrounded by covered galleries which looked into the courtyard. As well as providing access to the cloister ranges it was the canons' living area.

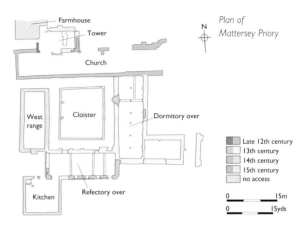

Plan of Mattersey Priory

N

Farmhouse
Tower
Church
West range
Cloister
Dormitory over
Kitchen
Refectory over

Late 12th century
13th century
14th century
15th century
no access

0   15m
0   15yds

¾ mile down rough drive, 1 mile E of Mattersey off B6045
OS Map 112, ref SK 703896

RUFFORD ABBEY

History

In 1146 Gilbert de Gaunt, Earl of Lincoln, founded the Cistercian abbey of St Mary the Virgin. The monks of this order, also known as the 'white monks' because of their habits of undyed wool, believed in the value of an austere life based upon prayer and hard work. Rufford Abbey was moderately wealthy and able to sustain a community of monks between its completion in about 1170 and its suppression in 1536.

Rufford was one of the first abbeys in England to be affected by the suppression of the monasteries, and the whole estate was quickly acquired by George Talbot, fourth Earl of Shrewsbury. The conversion of the west range of monastic buildings into a house (1560–90) was undertaken by the sixth earl, who was the fourth and final husband of the indomitable Bess of Hardwick, from whom he was then bitterly estranged. In 1610, a new projecting wing was added to the northern end of this range.

The estate was inherited in 1626 by Mary Talbot, sister of the seventh and eighth Earls of Shrewsbury, and it passed to her husband, George Savile. William Savile, George's successor, made Rufford Abbey the seat of the Savile family after he burnt down the Saviles' original home in order to prevent its being occupied

The 19th-century bridge leading to the house at Rufford Abbey

42

by a Parliamentarian garrison during the Civil War.

In 1679, the Savile family constructed a new north wing on the site of the abbey church, containing reception rooms and a long gallery. They also built the large stable block to the right of the house. The surviving roofed southern service wing (currently used as offices) was also added by the Saviles in the 17th century. In 1938, the third Baron Savile inherited the Rufford estate as a minor, but his trustees split it into lots and sold it off. The abbey and park were bought by Nottinghamshire County Council in 1952, and the north and east wings were demolished in 1956. The remaining west range and south service wing were put into the care of the Ministry of Works at the same date.

Description

The abbey is approached from the car park over the 19th-century Jacobean-style bridge. The roofed porch formed the original main entrance to the Earl of Shrewsbury's 16th-century house. The inner double doors lead into the now ruined Brick Hall, which formed a grand initial reception room for the post-suppression house.

This area of the building originally formed the lay brothers' dormitory. To the right is a fine late 14th-century window, with a surround of carved heads and foliage. Further to the right is the medieval night stair, which leads down from the ground-floor dormitory to the area of the cellar. Immediately in front of the night stair is a large area of open lawn – this was the location of the original abbey church and the 1670s northern wing of the house.

To the right is the entrance to the original cellar and monks' refectory. This cellar, a well-preserved example of Cistercian architecture, is plain with simple rounded and octagonal columns supporting the vaults. Traces of the day stair and of alcoves for holding the linen and spoons for use in the refectory can be seen in the far (front) wall.

A carved stone head in the abbey grounds

2 miles S of Ollerton off A614 OS Map 120, ref SK 646648 Open March–Dec: 10am–5pm daily; Jan–Feb: 10am–4pm daily; closed 25 Dec. For full details of opening times please call: 01623 822944

The West Midlands, like the East, are characterised by a rich and diverse heritage. The landscape in the south of the West Midlands features gently rolling hills, sweeping from the limestone of the Cotswolds through the Vale of Evesham to the clay slopes of Warwickshire. To the north, around Stoke-on-Trent, into the Staffordshire moorlands and the Peak District, steep peaks and plunging valleys complete England's transition from south to north.

Evidence of human occupation remains in such prehistoric monuments as Arthur's Stone, Herefordshire, probably used as a communal burial site and constructed some time after 3700 BC. Some 3,000 years later, an Iron Age community built the hill fort at Oswestry, Shropshire, and over the centuries its ramparts and earthworks were gradually extended until the site was abandoned with the arrival of the Romans.

From the seventh to the early ninth centuries AD, this region was under the control of the kingdom of Mercia. The Mercian kings constructed the great boundary earthworks, now known as Offa's Dyke, to divide the lands of the Anglo-Saxons from those of the Welsh kingdoms in the west. The development of border fortifications continued in later centuries. Clun Castle, Shropshire, for example, set high on a rock mound, was built in the late 11th century, originally in

Left: Moreton Corbet Castle, Shropshire, from the north

Facing page: Holy Trinity Church, Stratford-upon-Avon, Warwickshire

timber, to defend the valley route into Wales. Wigmore Castle, Herefordshire, was the stronghold of the powerful Mortimer family, from which they maintained control over parts of central Wales.

The destruction of the Civil War in the 17th century also had a lasting impact on many buildings in the region. In Shropshire, Parliamentarian forces captured and burned down Moreton Corbet Castle, and in 1645 they besieged the 12th-century Augustinian abbey of Lilleshall.

The West Midlands have associations with many historical figures in the arts and literature, of whom the playwright and poet William Shakespeare, born in Stratford-upon-Avon, is the most famous.

However, it is commerce, industry and scientific innovation that define so much of the region's later history, landscape and architecture. The West Midlands are rich in natural resources, from the clay of north Staffordshire to the iron ore of the Peak District and the coal of Shropshire, Warwickshire and Staffordshire. These deposits were exploited from the mid-18th century onwards, leading to the development of major mining and manufacturing industries and the expansion of towns such as Birmingham, Dudley, West Bromwich and Walsall, at the heart of the so-called 'Black Country'.

Alongside industrial development came technological and engineering innovation – the Iron Bridge, Shropshire, was the world's first, built in 1779 by the local ironmaster Abraham Darby. Now a World Heritage Site, it stands today as an international symbol of the Industrial Revolution.

An engraving of Lilleshall Abbey in 1731, by Samuel and Nathaniel Buck

Unstaffed sites
● *Staffed sites*

Croxden Abbey

STAFFORDSHIRE

Old Oswestry
Hill Fort

Moreton
Corbet Castle

*Haughmond
Abbey*

Lilleshall
Abbey

*Boscobel House &
the Royal Oak*

Wroxeter Roman City

*Buildwas
Abbey*

White Ladies
Priory

*Wall Roman Site
(Letocetum)*

Cantlop Bridge

Iron Bridge

Acton
Burnell
Castle

Wenlock Priory

Langley
Chapel

WEST
MIDLANDS

Mitchell's Fold
Stone Circle

Clun
Castle

Stokesay Castle

SHROPSHIRE

Halesowen
Abbey

Wigmore Castle

*Mortimer's Cross
Water Mill*

WORCESTERSHIRE

Witley Court

*Kenilworth
Castle*

Edvin Loach
Old Church

Leigh Court
Barn

WARWICKSHIRE

Arthur's
Stone

HEREFORDSHIRE

Rotherwas
Chapel

Longtown
Castle

● *Goodrich Castle*

47

IMAGINED LANDSCAPES

Many writers from the Midlands – even those who later sought their fortune elsewhere – have brought this region to international attention. Foremost, of course, is William Shakespeare, born in Stratford-upon-Avon, Warwickshire, in 1564. By the 1590s, he was established in London, but his young family remained in his native town; he always considered Stratford his home.

Many significant religious writers are associated with this region. John Wyclif, vicar of Lutterworth from 1374 to 1384, was the instigator of the translation into English of the most influential book of all, the Bible. John Foxe, from Boston, Lincolnshire, was a zealous Protestant, publishing his enduring *Book of Martyrs* in 1563. George Fox, born near Nuneaton, Warwickshire, became the founder of the Quakers, recording his spiritual search in his extraordinary *Journal* (1694).

In the field of secular writing, Anne Bradstreet left Boston

The Shakespeare Memorial in Stratford-upon-Avon

for Massachusetts in 1630. She was the first published woman poet in the New World, and her later poems appear in every anthology of American poetry. During the 18th and 19th centuries, two giants of British literature also left the Midlands. Samuel Johnson, the great lexicographer, grew up among the stock of his father's bookselling business in Lichfield, Staffordshire, but became famously attached to London life; and Alfred, Lord Tennyson, although associated with Somersby near Horncastle, Lincolnshire, spent only his early life there. The wildly romantic, notorious and prolific Lord Byron is more closely identified with the region. His teenage years were spent at Newstead Abbey, Nottinghamshire, and he returned there between his Mediterranean travels. He had drawn inspiration from the medieval monastic ruins but, deep in debt, he had to sell the property before he was 30. Six years later, in 1824, he was buried nearby at Hucknall.

One of Byron's friends, Sir Walter Scott, used two castles in the Midlands as settings for his novels: Kenilworth, Warwickshire, in his novel (1821) of that name about

WRITERS IN THE MIDLANDS

Amy Robsart, wife of Robert Dudley, Earl of Leicester, favourite of Elizabeth I; and Ashby de la Zouch, Leicestershire – the scene for the great tournament in *Ivanhoe* (1819) in which Richard the Lionheart defeated all the knights of his rebellious brother, John.

Scenes from contemporary Victorian life were described by Thomas Hughes in *Tom Brown's Schooldays* (1857), based upon his experiences at Rugby School, and were lyrically imagined by A. E. Housman in *A Shropshire Lad* (1896); the rural background of many of George Eliot's novels reflects her upbringing near Nuneaton. Earlier in the 19th century, the

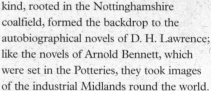

great pastoral poet John Clare, who spent much of his life in Northampton Asylum, had evoked the landscapes of his county, most successfully in *The Shepherd's Calendar* (1827).

Rural and urban realities of a different kind, rooted in the Nottinghamshire coalfield, formed the backdrop to the autobiographical novels of D. H. Lawrence; like the novels of Arnold Bennett, which were set in the Potteries, they took images of the industrial Midlands round the world. Similarly, Northamptonshire provided landscapes for some of the novels of H. E. Bates, and for those of J. L. Carr, staunch defender of medieval churches, one of which is the centrepiece of his novel *A Month in the Country* (1980).

Above: *Portrait of Lord Byron by Theodore Gericault*

Left: The Queen of the Tournament, *a scene from* Ivanhoe, *by Frank Topham*

ARTHUR'S STONE

History

Arthur's Stone is an important survival of a Neolithic chambered tomb, one of some 300 monuments of its type identified in the British Isles. It was used as a communal burial place, probably over many generations. The site, once covered by a high earth mound, was no doubt chosen for its prominent position looking across the Dore Valley to the Black Mountains beyond. At least two ancient roadways converged at this point. The site has traditionally been identified as the scene of one of King Arthur's battles, hence the name. The barrow actually dates from the early Neolithic period, some time after 3700 BC, when the first farmers were cultivating the land. Construction of such a sizeable monument demanded a communal effort by a large number

Arthur's Stone, a burial site once covered by an earth mound

of people. A Neolithic settlement was located nearby, on Dorstone Hill, from where flint tools, stone axes and pottery have been recovered. More stone tools were discovered at the barrow during repair work in 1900.

Description

The monument is constructed of locally quarried Old Red Sandstone. Most of the earth mound that once covered the tomb has been removed or eroded, leaving the stone structure exposed. From the edge of the former barrow, the remains of a stone-lined passage run east–west for 5m (16ft). It then turns at a right angle and extends southwards for almost 3m (10ft), before entering the burial chamber. The constriction in the passage just beyond the turn may indicate the point at which the entrance was originally blocked. The chamber is constructed of nine stones. Each stands to a height of 1.1m (3ft 6in), and five of them support a massive hexagonal capstone. This has now broken in

The massive capstone of the monument, supported by five standing stones

two places and has partly fallen, but was originally almost 6m (19ft) long, 3.7m (12ft) wide and 0.6m (2ft) thick. A huge effort would have been required to raise this 25-ton stone into position.

Some outlines of the original earth mound, which measured some 22m (72ft) by 19m (62ft), survive and suggest an oval shape orientated approximately east–west. The exposed kerbstones in the south-east quarter give an impression of its size. There is also a single standing stone to the south. Two further upright stones were probably once capped by a lintel stone to form a trilithon, or three-stone portal, on this side.

7 miles E of Hay-on-Wye, off B4348 near Dorstone OS Map 148, ref SO 319431

EDVIN LOACH OLD CHURCH

History

The curious name of this place originates in the late 11th century, when the district of Yedeven was divided between the Loges and Ralph families, hence the present names of the parishes of Edvin Loach and Edvin Ralph. The ruined church, once dedicated to St Giles but later known as St Mary's, probably dates back to this time. A 16th-century survey describes how the church 'adioygneth here so neere an owld decayed fortification as they both seeme to possesse … antiquity and poverty'. In fact, the church lies within the bailey (the outer defended area) of a Norman motte-and-bailey castle: the motte – a large conical mound on which a timber fortification stood – can still be clearly seen. The herringbone-pattern stonework on the north and south walls is a feature of early Norman churches in this part of England, as is the style of the simple south doorway.

In the 16th century, the church was apparently remodelled and the tower added. It continued in use until about 1860, when the new church (not in the care of English Heritage) was built. This is a small-scale but rather fine example of 19th-century church architecture designed in the Early English style by the great Victorian architect Sir George Gilbert Scott. The old church gradually became dilapidated, though its roof was still intact as late as the 1890s.

The remains of Edvin Loach Old Church seen from the graveyard

Description

The church has a simple layout, with a nave and a chancel. Locally quarried soft sandstone rubble was used to build the walls. The corners, and window and door edges, however, were carved from harder tufa – a type of carboniferous limestone found near calcareous springs. The two types of stone differ in colour and texture. Interesting features include the herringbone arrangement of the wall masonry, and the doorway with its bulky tufa lintel. This must have been rather a dark building, as it had narrow windows high in the walls – just the lower half of one 11th-century window survives by the south door. Like most early churches, it was modified in later centuries. The east wall and parts of the north and south walls were apparently rebuilt in the 12th century, while the buttresses at the junction between nave and chancel appear to be 13th-century additions. The Tudor-period tower, apparently always open to the nave, was built on two levels and lit by square-headed windows.

Outside the church, the boundary of the Norman castle bailey formed a roughly square enclosure about 70m (229ft) wide. It was surrounded by a ditch about 4m (13ft) wide, now visible as a shallow depression in the field to the south. The higher level of the graveyard, especially at its western end, is accounted for by many generations of burials in this small rural community.

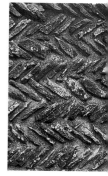

Above: Detail of the herringbone pattern of the stonework

Left: The interior of the church from the south-east

4 miles N of Bromyard on unclassified road off B4203
OS Map 149, ref SO 663584

LONGTOWN CASTLE

History

Ewias Lacey Castle, as it was once known, may have been built on an already well-defended site. Its prominent location, on a spur of high ground between two river valleys, and the evidence of its outer earthworks, suggest to some that an Iron Age camp may have been established here. The Romans also probably occupied the site. An alternative suggestion is that the origins of the site lie in the late Saxon period, in the 10th century.

The keep and curtain wall of Longtown Castle

What is certain is that in 1086 Domesday Book recorded the land here as belonging to the Lacey family, who exacted payments in honey and pigs from their tenants. The first castle on this site was a timber structure, perched on top of the man-made motte, or mound. In the 12th century, the Laceys spent the considerable sum of £37 improving this castle, and the present stone keep dates from about this time.

The Laceys, like other powerful families in the Welsh Marches, were medieval warlords. The English monarchs could not easily control them, but tolerated them in return for their support against the Welsh. In the 1230s, the Lacey lordship ended; the castle then passed through a number of owners but retained its importance. In 1233, Henry III visited, ordering the garrison to be enlarged. In 1403,

Henry IV, finding the castle somewhat decayed, commanded it to be refortified for defence against attacks led by the Welsh chieftain Owain Glyn Dwr. By the 1450s, however, it seems to have fallen out of use. Longtown, from which the castle now takes its name, was a planned medieval market town outside the castle ramparts. The town was not a success, perhaps as a result of the Black Death in the mid-14th century: it gradually shrank in size and importance to the small village seen today.

Description

This well-preserved Norman castle has the characteristic features of a steep-sided motte, 10m (33ft) high, at the north end and a bailey, or outer defended area, to the south. Visitors enter through a break in the curtain wall, which is perhaps a missing gatehouse. Some substantial parts of the curtain walls remain. The inner bailey is entered through the gatehouse, and the groove for the portcullis is clearly visible.

The most striking feature at Longtown is the stone keep on top of the motte, reached by a flight of steep steps. Round keeps were rare in England, though more common in Wales, and were late developments; they were structurally stronger and were easier to defend than square fortifications. The keep walls are 5m (16ft) thick, though its surviving shell is incomplete and unroofed. It was a two-storey structure over an undercroft, with the living accommodation on the upper floor. Notable features include the windows, possibly enlarged in the 14th century; a fireplace; corbels to support floor beams; and a projecting seven-seat latrine. The exterior originally had three semicircular projecting towers, one incorporating a chimney flue, and another containing a spiral stair. The design of the castle may have been relatively simple, but it was still a formidable structure. The mown path to the left of the steps to the keep gives a view, through the hedge, of the steep bank on which the curtain wall once sat.

The latrine projecting from the wall of the keep

4 miles WSW of Abbey Dore
OS Map 161, ref SO 321291

ROTHERWAS CHAPEL

History

For over six centuries, Rotherwas Chapel was an integral part of a sizeable manor house, the seat of the De La Barre and later the Bodenham families. Nearby is the site of successive houses: the medieval half-timbered mansion, its stone-built Tudor extension (with elaborate formal gardens) and its Georgian

Rotherwas Chapel, seen from the west

successor, built in 1732 but itself demolished in 1926 (following the death of the last of the Bodenhams).

Surviving documents record in 1304 a chapel of ease at Rotherwas, for nearby Dinedor Church. In 1483, the estate passed by marriage from the De La Barre family to the Bodenhams, and in the 1580s Sir Roger Bodenham enlarged the house and rebuilt the chapel. Sir Roger was converted to Roman Catholicism in 1606, apparently following a 'miraculous' cure of 'a gross tumour in the legs', and thereafter the chapel was used for worship by local Roman Catholics. As Royalists, the family suffered after the Civil War, and their estate was confiscated. By 1732, however, their fortunes had revived sufficiently to enable Sir Charles Bodenham to replace the old house with a grand mansion. The chapel's west tower was rebuilt in this period. The outhouses, barn and stable block also survive.

The chapel interior was updated in 1868, when Charles Bodenham commissioned Edward Welby Pugin (the son of A. W. N. Pugin, architect of the Houses of Parliament) to embellish the chapel. A few years later, Bodenham's widow, Irene, employed Edward's younger brother, Peter Paul Pugin, to extend the east end. Fortunately, the chapel survived the demolition of the house, and was taken into the guardianship of the state in 1928.

Description

Externally, features from different periods can still be seen, including the chapel's medieval and Tudor sandstone core, the Georgian tower, and the Victorian spire and porch. The interior features the same mixture of parts from different dates, from the 14th-century north nave windows to the Victorian chancel, sanctuary and south-east chapel. The western three bays of the church form the nave as reconstructed by Sir Roger Bodenham in about 1589. This date is inscribed on one of the roof beams to commemorate the birth of Sir Roger's son Thomas. The ornamental Elizabethan roof comprises a complex scheme of tie-beams, arched braces and pendants. The former west gallery, which held the lord of the manor's pew, has a blocked fireplace. The south window of the chapel depicts in detail Sir Roger Bodenham's pilgrimage, his cure from disease and his conversion to Roman Catholicism.

The Pugins' Victorian additions, including the elaborate decoration of the east window, altar, screen and lower walls, are the chapel's most striking features. The east window has portrait figures of Charles and Irene Bodenham. The apsidal sanctuary has a restored tiled floor and elaborate reredos behind the carved wooden altar. On the north side, a door leads to the vestry – complete with ornate chimney and fireplace – and the pinewood confessional, entered from the nave. The south-east chapel was built by Irene Bodenham to house her husband's, and later her own, tomb, though the remains of both were removed in 1912.

1 1/2 miles SE
of Hereford
on B4399
Keykeeper
located at
nearby filling
station
OS Map 149,
ref SO 536383

57

WIGMORE CASTLE

Facing page: Wigmore Castle, the subject of an extensive programme of conservation in the 1990s

History

Hidden above the little village of Wigmore are the ruins of one of the largest castles along the Welsh border. The original motte-and-bailey castle was built by William FitzOsbern, one of William the Conqueror's captains at the Battle of Hastings. It was one of a series of castles designed by the Normans to defend England against attack by the Welsh. It soon passed into the hands of the powerful Mortimer family and became the chief fortress from which they controlled large parts of central Wales.

Although some of the surviving stonework is earlier, much of the castle seems to have been rebuilt in the 14th century by Roger Mortimer, perhaps

Engraving of the castle by Samuel and Nathaniel Buck, 1732

the family's best-known figure. Roger became virtual ruler of England after he and his lover, Isabella, Edward II's estranged queen, had engineered the king's deposition and murder in 1327. However, Roger's influence over the young Edward III was brief, and he was executed in 1330 at Edward's instigation.

The Mortimers continued to be players on the national stage before Wigmore eventually passed to Richard, Duke of York, in 1424 and ultimately to Edward IV. But the castle was rarely used, and was partly ruinous by the 16th century, when it was sold by Elizabeth I to the Harleys of nearby Brampton Bryan. Although Sir Robert Harley technically held it for Parliament in the Civil War, it was made indefensible to prevent Royalist forces using it. The medieval castle was therefore left remarkably undisturbed. After several centuries of neglect, a conservation programme was undertaken in the 1990s (see pp. 60–61). Its aim was to consolidate rather than restore the structure, and to ensure that the castle's natural environment was preserved. Much of the castle still remains buried up to first-floor level.

Description

From the footpath, visitors cross the castle's outer bailey, of which only earthworks remain. At the foot of the hill, the path to the right gives a good view of the defensive ditch and the curtain wall. Back at the gate, steps lead across the ditch separating the outer bailey from the rest of the castle, and up to the gatehouse, now half submerged in its own rubble. The early 14th-century curtain wall, extending from either side of the gatehouse, includes three surviving residential towers, two to the left and one, the east tower, to the right.

From the east tower, steps lead to the raised area that contained the main domestic buildings of the castle. On the right are the earthwork and stone remains of a huge rectangular hall. There was a chamber block, or two-storey living quarters, at the

far end. A half-octagonal tower completed this range.

Further steep steps lead up into the inner bailey on top of the motte, where the curtain wall on the north side survives to its full height. At the far west end is the keep, with only its stair turret visible above ground. From the steps up to the grassy top can be seen the great ditch, part natural and part man-made, that separates the castle from the ridge beyond. In the valley to the north is Wigmore Abbey, where the Mortimers are buried. From the platform in the tower on the east side of the motte, there is a panoramic view over the castle, as well as the church and village below.

There are steep steps to the summit, which are hazardous in icy conditions. Children must stay under close control and should not climb the walls or banks. Strong footwear is recommended. There is no custodial presence.

8 miles W of Ludlow on A4110. ¾ mile from Wigmore village, via footpath off Castle Street
OS Map 148, ref SO 408693

59

Wigmore Castle remained an untouched ruin into the 1990s, buried within the rubble of its own collapse. Since the 17th century, the castle has been managed as woodland pasture. Although many parts of the building were stable, others threatened to fall, and some repair was essential if the castle was to survive. English Heritage became responsible for the site in 1995 and instigated a programme of conservation that aimed to minimise the effects of repair.

At many historic sites, the plants and other organisms that colonise ruins have been stripped away during conservation. Fallen masonry has sometimes been

removed to reveal once-buried remains of buildings. To do this at Wigmore – a dignified ruin that can be explored in its mature landscape – would have destroyed the elements that make the site special.

A dense grass matting protecting the fragile masonry originally covered the castle walls. Ivy had almost completely concealed other parts; scrub, young saplings and blackthorn made access difficult and threatened the upstanding masonry. Trees growing in the walls had caused serious cracking and allowed water to permeate, causing a large part of the south curtain wall to fall in 1988. Removal of stone for reuse in local buildings had also stripped the inner face of most of the curtain wall. A balance was required between leaving what was beneficial to the fabric and removing the underlying causes of instability.

The philosophy of repair was to leave the ruin much as it appeared in 1995, after a full survey had been carried out. To establish the causes of instability, archaeologists excavated in only two areas to minimise ground disturbance: the south curtain wall between

Aerial view of Wigmore Castle in 1989, before conservation

the south and south-west towers, and the east tower. Initially, the protective grass covering of the walls was temporarily removed to an on-site nursery. (Only the ivy was not retained.) Archaeologists then recorded the walls and towers, and a new grass capping was created. As work progressed, investigators found that walls could be stabilised simply by lifting back the grass where facing stones were loose to reset them. Cracks were 'stitched' with threaded stainless-steel rods, and overhanging masonry underpinned with matching local stone. Stainless steel was also used to support rubble exposed after the removal of dressed stones from windows and doors. The outer face of the fallen south curtain wall was rebuilt to match the masonry to either side. The basement of the south tower was not conserved, as it is an important bat roost.

The care taken in minimising the effects of conservation of the fabric carried over into the site presentation. Safety railings of untreated oak were installed only where blackthorn could not be used to protect visitors from dangerous areas, and walls were heightened to a safe level where the only alternative would have been an intrusive fence. Timber steps were laid in or on the topsoil so that they would not compromise the site's buried archaeology, and handrails were designed to be both safe and unobtrusive. Cutting down the grass in areas where visitors had always walked created a natural route around the site. As a result, the castle looks little different now from how it appeared before work started, but access has been improved and the ecology enhanced by careful management.

Above: The walls retain their protective grass matting

Right: The gatehouse, buried within its own rubble

ACTON BURNELL CASTLE

History

The Burnell family of Acton Burnell held land in Shropshire from the 1180s, though it was a century later that Robert Burnell came to prominence. Entering royal service as a clerk to Henry III's son Prince Edward, he rose to become Chancellor of England and Bishop of Bath and Wells when the prince acceded to the throne as Edward I in 1272. The king's military campaigns in Wales frequently brought him to Shropshire, and he stayed at Acton. His visit in 1283 assumed national significance when he held a parliament, according to tradition, in the tithe barn here; this was supposedly the first at which commoners were represented.

In 1284, Robert Burnell obtained a licence from the king to fortify his residence. Work was probably still in progress when Robert died in 1292. The large first-floor windows of the castle suggest, however, that it never had a serious defensive purpose and that it was instead perhaps designed to impress. Evidence of Robert's building zeal may also be seen in the adjacent church, a fine example of Early English architecture. Burnell's wealth and his position as bishop enabled him to employ the best masons. By 1420, however, the castle was abandoned. It was allowed to decay while a new house, Acton Burnell Hall (not in the care of English Heritage), was built next to it in the 18th century. Thus saved from later alterations, the castle remains an impressive example of a medieval fortified manor house.

Acton Burnell Castle from the west – the south-west tower was converted into a dovecote in the 18th century

Description

St Mary's Church (not in the care of English Heritage) lies near the castle, as do the remains of the tithe barn and the now-buried foundations of other domestic structures. An important household such as the bishop's needed ample accommodation for staff, guests and attendants, as well as stables, bakehouses and breweries to cater for a large number of occupants.

The red-coursed sandstone remains of Robert Burnell's residence dominate the site. It resembles a Norman keep, with two central storeys under a twin-span roof, and four battlemented projecting corner towers. In the 18th century a pyramid roof was added to the south-west tower to convert it into a dovecote.

The living accommodation, lit by large traceried windows, was at first-floor level. Life here revolved around a large, nearly square, hall at the eastern end, divided by an open arcade running east–west. This hall was entered directly from the outside via steps, now demolished. West of the

The interior of the castle, showing the door and window openings

hall were private chambers over three storeys, with access to the latrine block; its central projecting structure is also adorned by a pyramid roof.

The ground floor of the castle contained storage and service rooms. The entrance was originally on the east side, where at least two of the three doorways connected with other, mainly timber-framed buildings. Apart from the end walls of the barn, just visible in the private grounds, nothing of these buildings survives above ground, though there is evidence on the east wall of the castle for a two-storey structure.

In Acton Burnell, signposted from A49, 8 miles S of Shrewsbury
OS Map 126, ref SJ 534019

63

CANTLOP BRIDGE

History

A bridge for horses once carried the road from Shrewsbury to Acton Burnell across Cound Brook, but in 1812 this was replaced by an iron bridge for carriages. There is, however, some doubt about the date of the bridge – an iron plate with the inscription 'Thomas Telford Esqr, Engineer, 1818' was once attached to the structure, and it may be a replacement for an earlier bridge that failed. The historical interest of the bridge lies in this association with the

Cantlop Bridge, probably designed by the pioneering engineer Thomas Telford

great Scottish engineer. Telford was County Surveyor of Shropshire from 1787 to 1834 and designed some 42 bridges for the county. Of these, just seven were cast iron, of which only this one survives. It is not certain that Telford personally designed the bridge, as he did not list it in his autobiography. It appears, however, to be a scaled-down version of the bridge he did design at Meole Brace, Shropshire, which was demolished in 1933.

A portrait of Thomas Telford by William Brockedon (1834)

Telford was the first engineer to demonstrate how light, cast-iron frames could facilitate the building of bridges with flatter profiles and less substantial foundations. His development of single-span iron bridges was a turning point in bridge design and engineering. In the 1960s, Cantlop Bridge was found to have cracks, and was closed to traffic. At this time a new road bridge was built immediately to the west.

Description

Cantlop is a single-span bridge of painted iron supporting a roadway on metal plates, which have been tarmacked and gravelled over. The span of the bridge is 9.5m (31ft). The painted railings have replaced the original parapets and perhaps slightly disrupt the intended harmonious design. At either end, the arch is supported by sandstone and brick-faced abutments.

The main interest of the bridge lies in its iron superstructure, comprising a lattice of four ribs, braced by five cross-members. It illustrates how Telford used the strength of cast iron to construct bridges with a relatively flat profile. It makes an interesting comparison with Abraham Darby's 1779 bridge at Coalbrookdale (see pp. 70–73), which has a free-standing semicircular arch supporting the bridge deck. Telford's arches are flat, and rest on splayed abutments.

3/4 mile SW of Berrington on unclassified road off A458
OS Map 126, ref SJ 517062

THOMAS TELFORD

Memorably dubbed 'The Colossus of Roads' by the poet Robert Southey, Thomas Telford was one of Britain's greatest engineers. He was responsible for thousands of miles of canals and roads, as well as bridges and buildings, in Britain and on the Continent, many of which are still in use today.

Telford was born in Westerkirk, Dumfries-shire, in 1757, the son of a shepherd. After he left the local parish school, he was apprenticed to a stonemason, and educated himself by reading books borrowed from the local gentry. He also learned to draw by sketching architecture. In 1782 he moved to London where he was employed as a stonemason on the construction of Somerset House, designed by Sir William Chambers, and met William Pulteney, who became his most important patron. In 1787 Telford went to Shropshire to work on the restoration of Shrewsbury Castle. In that year, he became County Surveyor of Public Works, a position he retained until his death. In Shropshire, he worked on road improvements, bridges, private houses and the restoration of churches such as St Mary's, Shrewsbury.

In 1793 Telford was appointed surveyor and engineer to the Ellesmere Canal, connecting the rivers Mersey, Dee and Severn. One of his best-known structures was the Pontcysyllte Aqueduct across the narrow valley of the Dee in north Wales. Completed in 1805, the aqueduct is 38.4m

Drawing by Thomas Malton of a proposed single-span London Bridge designed by Thomas Telford

(126ft) high and 307m (1,007ft) long, with 18 masonry piers supporting a cast-iron trough containing the canal. It was described by Sir Walter Scott as 'the most impressive work of art [he had] ever seen'. In the same period, Telford advised on the construction of harbour works, docks and piers, including many in his native Scotland. He was also responsible for the Caledonian Canal built across the Highlands in 1804–22, which in its construction used the most advanced technology of the time, including iron railways and steam engines for pumping and dredging. From 1803, he was also engineer to the Highland Road Commissioners, constructing more than 1,000 miles of roads and bridges in Scotland. Other achievements in road-building were the Bangor to Chester and London to Holyhead routes. Road bridges such as that at Buildwas, Shropshire (1796), used innovative cast-iron construction that enabled wider spans and lighter structures. Telford proposed a cast-iron bridge over the River Thames as a replacement for London Bridge, although this was never executed. His masterpiece was the wrought-iron Menai Bridge linking

Mythe Bridge, Twyning, Gloucestershire, built in 1826–30

the island of Anglesey with the Welsh mainland. When it opened in 1826, it was the world's longest suspension bridge, and its design widely influenced those of later great engineers. The Conwy suspension bridge was completed in the same year, and retains its original ironwork.

Telford listed his works in his autobiography, which he began in 1831, three years before his death. His reputation declined with the arrival of the railways, but was revived with the advent of the motor car. His name is commemorated in a new town, Telford, Shropshire, which was developed in the 1950s.

History

The remains of Clun Castle sit high on a natural rocky mound in a loop of the River Clun, on the edge of the village of the same name. This quiet, picturesque settlement was planned in the 12th century and was laid out on a regular grid. It grew into a flourishing village with annual fairs and a market.

Clun Castle, rebuilt in stone in the 13th century

The original motte-and-bailey castle here was built in the late 11th century, probably by Picot de Say, one of William the Conqueror's followers. It may have been built of wood. The castle was intended to guard the valley route into Wales and to demonstrate the authority of the English monarchy in the border region. It was also the administrative centre of the Barony of Clun.

William Fitz Alan of Oswestry acceded to the Clun lordship in 1155. Under the Fitz Alans, the castle suffered a number of attacks: in 1196, Rhys, prince of south Wales, captured the castle and burned it down. King John sent troops when John Fitz Alan joined the revolt against him in 1215, and the castle withstood a later siege by Llewellyn in 1233.

The 13th and 14th centuries were the castle's heyday, when the rich Fitz Alans used it as a residence and

hunting lodge: they probably rebuilt it in stone in the late 13th century. Edward I spent the night of 18 June 1295 here. But in the early 15th century devastation around Clun by followers of Owain Glyn Dwr, self-styled prince of Wales, brought an end to this period of prosperity. The castle continued in use as a hunting lodge, but was no longer the Fitz Alans' main residence, and by 1539 it was described as 'somewhat ruinous'. It played no part in the Civil War, and was eventually bought by the Dukes of Norfolk, descendants of the medieval Fitz Alans.

Description

The site is dominated today by the four-storey great tower, built into the side of the motte, or mound. A section of the curtain wall with two flanking, half-round towers also survives from this bailey, or courtyard, together with two further baileys enclosed by massive earthworks. The castle farm was within the smallest bailey, where the bowling green is now situated. The towers and curtain wall, built of the same rubblestone as the great tower, appear to date probably from the late 13th century. The earthworks of medieval gardens are visible in the valley just across the river.

The great tower provided living accommodation for the lord, his family and his guests, with the grandest room on the top floor; smaller private rooms were set within the thickness of the wall. The tower was at least 28m (90ft) high, with flat buttresses supporting the northern corners. There are slits through which defending archers could fire (though some are dummy slits), and many round-headed windows. Although the tower was built about 1300, its design seems to have been intended deliberately to echo that of the great Norman keeps of the 12th century.

The great tower of the castle, built into the side of a huge earth mound

In Clun, off A488, 18 miles W of Ludlow
OS Map 137, ref SO 299809

The world's first iron bridge was cast in Coalbrookdale by the local ironmaster Abraham Darby and erected across the River Severn in 1779. Set in a spectacular wooded gorge, it is now part of a World Heritage Site, and is Britain's best-known industrial monument.

Although this symbol of the Industrial Revolution sits in what is today a rural area, in the late 18th century this part of Shropshire was an industrial powerhouse because of its rich coal deposits near the surface. In 1709, Abraham Darby I, a former brass founder from Bristol, had begun

Iron Bridge, the first bridge in the world to be constructed of iron

to smelt local iron ore with coke made from Coalbrookdale coal. The expansion of industrial activity here in the upper Severn gorge, however, was handicapped without a bridge, the nearest being at Buildwas 3km (2 miles) away. Intense barge traffic along the river also required a single-span bridge, as the steep sides of the gorge ruled out rising approaches to a stone central arch.

It was the Shrewsbury architect Thomas Pritchard who first suggested in 1773 to the ironmaster John Wilkinson that an iron bridge be built over the Severn. The chosen crossing point, where a ferry had crossed from Benthall to Madeley Wood, had the advantage of high approaches on both sides and relative stability. Pritchard drew up the designs, but he died in 1777, a month after work had begun on a single-span bridge of 30m (100ft 6in) with five main semicircular ribs. Abraham Darby III, grandson of the first foundry owner, agreed to continue the project, and all the iron was cast at his Coalbrookdale

The construction methods are based on those used for woodworking

furnace. Construction was completed in 1779, using in all 378 tons of iron, and the world's first iron bridge was formally opened on New Year's Day 1781, having cost over £6,000.

Recent discoveries have shed much light on how the bridge was actually built. In 1997, a small watercolour sketch of the bridge under construction was discovered in a Stockholm museum. Together with recent research this has revealed much about the building process and has overturned earlier assumptions. It is now known that 70 per cent of the components – including all the large castings – were made individually to fit, and as a result each is slightly different from the others. Darby's workers employed woodworking joints – mortises and tenons, dovetails and wedges – and adapted them to the different properties of cast iron. A half-size replica of the main section of the bridge was built in 2001 as part of the research.

The bridge had a far-reaching impact on the local society and economy. It was always intended as a monument to the achievements of Shropshire ironmasters as well as a river crossing – it was an advertisement that gave their ironworks a competitive edge over their rivals'. The settlement that became known as Ironbridge quickly began to grow around the bridge after it had opened.

The development of a single-span cast-iron bridge also represented a turning point in British bridge design and engineering, and cast iron became widely used in the construction of bridges, aqueducts and buildings. The original builders, however, employing what was then new technology, had used much more

View of the Iron Bridge by William Williams (1780)

iron than was necessary. The engineer Thomas Telford subsequently recognised that lighter cast-iron frames, such as that used at Cantlop Bridge (see pp. 64–5), would allow the use of flatter profiles and less substantial foundations, while still enabling single spans and so avoiding the central piers that previously hindered river navigation.

The bridge's great weight accounts for its massive strength over the years: it resisted the severe flooding of 1795 without damage. By then, however, there had already been some trouble with the enormous stone abutments, which caused cracks in the ironwork when the river banks shifted slowly over time. The south abutment was modified several times and eventually replaced, initially by two wooden land arches and in 1821 by cast-iron arches.

The bridge remained in full use for over 150 years, by ever-increasing traffic. It was finally closed to vehicles in 1934, when it was designated an Ancient Monument. Further massive works to strengthen the bridge have been undertaken since to counteract the constant tendency of the gorge sides to push inwards: in 1973 a reinforced concrete strut was built across the bed of the river to brace the two abutments. English Heritage, together with the Ironbridge Gorge Museums Trust, carried out a full archaeological survey, record and analysis of the bridge in 1999–2000. The three-dimensional digital record now enables detailed understanding and management of the structure.

The Iron Bridge today lies at the heart of a renowned complex of living history museums, and visitors can still cross it on foot. There is an exhibition about its history in the brick tollhouse, which sits on the west side of the south abutment: the original tollhouse structure is contemporary with the bridge, and was extended in the mid-19th century. The Museum of the Gorge, north of the river, provides an excellent introduction to the history of the gorge as a whole.

In Ironbridge, 5 miles S of Telford, adjacent to A4169
OS Map 127, ref SJ 672034

73

Langley Chapel, viewed from the east

History

The Burnells of nearby Acton Burnell (see pp. 62–3) were lords of the manor of Langley, and in 1313 Richard Burnell obtained permission to build a chapel here. The structure of the present building dates from this time. In 1377, the manor of Langley passed to the Lee family, who fitted out the chapel in about 1546. In 1591, Sir Humphrey Lee moved to Langley. He was probably responsible for re-roofing the chapel in 1601 – a date given on the nave roof – and refurnishing it a few years later. By 1700 the chapel had largely fallen out of use, and thus escaped any attempt to re-order the interior according to the more elaborate 'High Church' model favoured in the 19th century. The last regular service was held here in 1871.

Description

Langley Chapel has a simple rectangular plan. It is built of dressed grey sandstone with a stone-tile roof, and has a small weatherboarded bell tower at the west end. On the exterior, the south wall has two Tudor doorways with flat arches and nail-studded doors. Inside is a variety of rather plain windows: one is square-headed, while others were perhaps remodelled from earlier medieval windows. Characteristically Tudor decoration of roses and fleurs-de-lis appears on the plaster frieze between the roof and south wall, although the corresponding frieze opposite has been lost. Glazed and decorated medieval tiles have been reused on the chancel floor.

It is the set of early 17th-century church fittings that makes Langley significant. The focus of worship in medieval churches was a raised stone altar set against the east wall. The central celebration was the 'sacrifice' of the Mass at the altar by a robed priest speaking in Latin. After the Reformation, however, the emphasis changed to preaching and reading the scriptures in English. Pulpits loomed large, sometimes literally, though at Langley the pulpit was relatively small and movable. The reading desk on the north side, however, is large, with seats inside and, unusually, a roof.

With the replacement in the Church of England of the Catholic mass by the Protestant communion service, a simple communion table replaced the stone altar. (The original communion table at Langley was stolen; the present one is a copy.) Seats were arranged round the table, appropriate for people sharing a meal, as at the Last Supper. The manner of receiving the bread and wine at communion was a matter of theological dispute.

At Langley, the furnishings allowed communicants to choose. Puritans could sit, while those who wished to could kneel.

The fittings of the chapel were designed to cater for social as well as theological gradations. The largest of the ornate box pews, intended for the Lee family, were placed at the front. Behind these were smaller box pews for farmers and tradespeople, while servants and labourers sat on benches at the back. At the west end is a raised desk for musicians.

Below: The interior of the church, which retains its early 17th-century fittings

1½ miles S of Acton Burnell, on unclassified road off A49; 9½ miles S of Shrewsbury
OS Map 149, ref SO 663584
Open
1 Mar–31 Oct: 10am–5pm daily; 1 Nov–28 Feb: 10am–4pm daily

Above: The ornate arch leading from the church to the cloister

Facing page: Plan of Lilleshall Abbey

Below: The west end of the church

History

But for its conversion into a fortified stronghold during the Civil War, more might have survived of this 12th-century Augustinian abbey. As it is, the extensive sandstone remains give an idea of its past magnificence.

Lilleshall was founded in about 1148 for a group of Arrouaisians, part of the wider congregation of Augustinian canons. The black canons, so called because of the colour of their habits, were communities of priests following a monastic rule but also preaching in churches and undertaking other parish work. The size and quality of the monastic complex at Lilleshall suggest that the abbey had rich and powerful benefactors.

In the 13th century Lilleshall prospered, and Henry III was entertained here twice in about 1240. The abbey derived income from gifts and legacies, farmland, two watermills and investments in property, as well as tolls for the use of Atcham Bridge over the River Severn.

During the early 14th century, however, Lilleshall had a financial crisis. The abbot was accused of mismanagement, and finances were also undermined by the reckless selling of corrodies, or pensions, to lay people. Although stability was restored, the number of canons had fallen to 10 or 11 by 1400, and at the suppression of the monasteries in 1538 there were nine canons and 43 servants, including a schoolmaster.

During the Civil War, Lilleshall was fortified by a Royalist garrison. After a siege of several weeks in 1645 Parliamentarian troops forced entry and caused much damage to the church. The abbey was then left to decay, and in the late 18th century a canal was cut through the precinct. Lilleshall was placed in guardianship in 1950, and was subsequently repaired and consolidated.

Description

In plan, Lilleshall follows the typical layout of a monastery, with its buildings arranged round a central cloister. The church is on the north side. Entering through its finely carved west doorway there is a clear view of the nave through to the presbytery. The doorway to the left reveals steep and dark stairs, from the top of which there is a fine view. The foundations of the stone screens dividing the eastern end of the church (used by the canons) from the nave are visible today. The great east window was inserted in the 14th century.

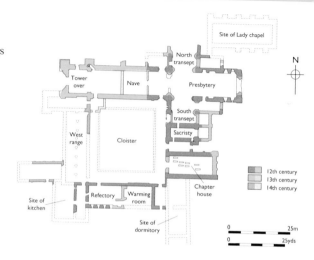

The processional door from the church into the cloister incorporates elaborate chevron decoration. The cloister, a place for quiet contemplation, reading and study, was perhaps where in the early 15th century the canon John Merk wrote his religious works, one of which was printed by William Caxton in 1483 in *The Golden Legend*.

The east range contained the sacristy, for sacred vessels, and the chapter house, where the canons met daily; inside are the gravestones of a number of Lilleshall's abbots. On the south side is the refectory, which is entered through a large arched doorway at its west end and lit by Romanesque-style windows. In the 14th century, the room was divided to provide a warming room in its eastern half, with a large fireplace by which the monks could warm themselves. On the west side, low walls survive of the abbot's private lodging.

On unclassified road off A518, 4 miles N of Oakengates
OS Map 127, ref 737143
Open
1 Apr–30 Sep: 10am–5pm

MITCHELL'S FOLD STONE CIRCLE

History

There are some 250 surviving stone circles in the British Isles, mostly situated in upland areas of the west. Of these, only about one-tenth are large, regular formations like that at Mitchell's Fold. Archaeological finds suggest that most stone circles date from the Late Neolithic period to the Middle Bronze Age, about 2400 to 1000 BC. Mitchell's Fold is most likely to date from the Early Bronze Age, about 2000 BC. At this time, scattered communities lived by farming and hunting, and the monument is small enough to have been built by a single community. There were two other circles nearby, Hoarstones, to the north-west, and Whetstones (now destroyed); a few miles south was a prehistoric axe-making centre at Cwm Mawr, from where stone axe-hammers were distributed as far afield as Land's End in Cornwall.

Stone circles probably held a ritual or religious significance for the communities that erected them. They were frequently associated with burial sites, and the remains of a cairn, or burial mound, can be found here near the outlying standing stone just to the south-east. They may also have been used to mark the seasons or to forecast significant lunar or solar events. The elusive purpose of these circles, together with their often remote and beautiful locations, has lent them an air of mystery and has given them a place in folklore. At Mitchell's Fold a magic cow was said

Mitchell's Fold Stone Circle, probably constructed in about 2000 BC

to give milk to all, until one night a witch drained her dry through a sieve. The cow vanished forthwith and, according to the legend, the witch was turned into the central stone and the circle erected to keep her in.

Description

The stones are reached by a walk of about 230m (250yd) from the parking area at the end of the track. Follow the waymarked trail straight ahead. The site lies at a height of about 300m (960ft) on a high saddle of land between Stapley Hill to the north and Corndon Hill to the south. The stones, which were brought from Stapley Hill, are all of the geological type known as dolerite.

Today 15 stones are visible: two lie flat, while the rest stand to an average height of nearly 0.5m (1ft 8in). Originally there were probably 30 stones. They formed a rough circle about 30m (100ft) in diameter, with one side noticeably flattened, probably deliberately, as this feature is quite common elsewhere. A single

Two of the remaining standing stones

stone stood at the centre of the circle, though its remains are now hidden below ground.

From the site panel, the path to the south-east leads to the outlying stone standing 0.7m (2ft 3in) high on a small prominence. The nearby mound is thought to be the remains of the cairn, from which stone has been removed. There are also various banks and depressions both within the circle and outside its perimeter. These are evidence of a later field system, probably early medieval. The land was ploughed in strips, leaving the typical ridge-and-furrow patterns.

16 miles SW of Shrewsbury
OS Map 137, ref SO 306984
Tel: 01939 232771

History

Shortly after the Norman Conquest a small fortified house, protected by a timber rampart and a ditch, was built at Moreton Toret, as this site was then known. In about 1239, the Corbet family acquired the site by marriage. They built a stone castle in the tradition of other fortified residences along the Welsh Marches.

In the 16th century, the castle was ambitiously remodelled in two phases. The first phase in 1538, under Sir

The Elizabethan south range of Moreton Corbet Castle

Andrew Corbet, included refacing the gatehouse and building a new east range. The second phase, the south range, is dated 1579, the year Sir Andrew died – the south-east corner bears the inscription ER21 (the 21st year of Elizabeth I's reign) – and incorporated the east range. Built over part of the filled-in moat, the new range was almost certainly begun by Sir Andrew's eldest son, Robert, ambassador to Antwerp. According to the antiquary William Camden, Robert, 'with an affectionate delight of Architecture, began to build … a most gorgeous and stately house, after the Italian model'. An ambitious formal garden was also planned. Robert died in 1583, and the house was completed by his younger brothers Richard and Vincent.

During the Civil War, Sir Vincent Corbet fortified the house in support of Charles I and provided it with a garrison of 110 men. Nevertheless, it was captured and set ablaze by a small force of Parliamentarian troopers, who tricked the Royalists into surrender after a minor skirmish in the dead of night. The marks left by musket shot are still visible. The house was restored after the Civil War by Sir Vincent Corbet, but it became derelict after 1700 and was partly demolished.

Detail of the 16th-century building in Architecture of the Renaissance in England (1894) by J. A. Gotch

Description

By entering through the gatehouse it is possible to appreciate how the Corbet family modernised the old castle by building against the curtain wall. The fireplaces on the left probably relate to Sir Andrew Corbet's great hall. On the right was the 16th-century kitchen. Much of the original curtain wall has been demolished or reduced in height. The bailey may once have been partly filled with timber buildings, of which no traces remain. On the first floor of the three-storey great tower there is a fireplace with decorated capitals. The doorway opened from a lost building tucked into the corner of the keep and the curtain wall.

Leaving the courtyard and walking clockwise around the outer circuit of the curtain wall, visitors arrive at the remains of the Elizabethan south range. The inspiration for the house very clearly came from Flemish buildings of the period, and the grandeur and symmetry of the design can still be appreciated from the south facade, which incorporates Classical columns in a riotous decorative display. The most notable surviving features inside are a large decorated fireplace and a vaulted brick cellar.

Nearby St Bartholomew's Church (not in the care of English Heritage) contains some fine tombstone effigies of the Corbets.

In Moreton Corbet, off B5063; 7 miles NE of Shrewsbury
OS Map 126, ref SJ 561231

81

OLD OSWESTRY HILL FORT

History

The site of this hill fort was perhaps continuously used for almost 1,000 years. As early as the ninth century BC the flattish top of the hill, protected by a wooden palisade, may have provided prehistoric communities with a stockade for animals. Archaeologists have also identified the sites of Bronze Age round huts, and a pottery crucible for bronzeworking found here suggests some small-scale industrial activity. By the early Iron Age, during the sixth century BC, the first significant earthwork fortifications were in place around the perimeter. These were constructed using boulders, some of which may be seen protruding from the bank. By this period, the area within the boundary probably had a relatively large population, living in round, stone-walled houses.

Over the following centuries, these earthworks were progressively rebuilt and extended. Two inturned entrances opposite each other were created, and the number of ramparts with ditches grew outwards from the initial two to five or, in places, seven. This hill fort may have been a stronghold of the local Cornovii tribe, and the progressive strengthening of the defences perhaps indicated power struggles between rival elites. With the arrival of the Romans, the site was largely abandoned. Later it was incorporated into Wat's Dyke, a defensive system 61km (38 miles) long, to the east and north of the more famous Offa's Dyke. Wat's Dyke may date from the fifth century AD. During the First World War, the hill fort was used as a training area for Canadian troops.

View of Old Oswestry Hill Fort, looking south, with Oswestry town beyond

Description

The hill fort looms over the skyline of Oswestry town, commanding far-reaching views over the surrounding countryside, and is still an impressive monument despite human depredations and erosion caused by centuries of wind and rain. Perhaps surprisingly, the mound of clay-capped sands, gravels and boulders from which the fort was created is not high, at only 168m (551ft) above sea level, which may explain the formidable size of the ramparts. These are among the most impressive of any British hill fort, enclosing a central area of 8.4ha (21 acres).

For centuries, the slopes of the hill fort were densely covered by trees, and an 18th-century writer describes threading his way 'through the thorny intricacies of this sylvan labyrinth'. At the base of the hill, the outermost earthworks are the most recent. There are five sets of ramparts, which are in places over 6m (19ft) high, with associated ditches. The remains are less visible on the steep eastern side of the hill, where soil slippage has caused them to merge into a more-or-less continuous slope. They are highest near the impressive western entrance, where two additional ramparts enclose a series of deep rectangular hollows. A feature unique to Old Oswestry Hill Fort, these may have been intended as storage pits, water cisterns or just additional fortifications designed to confuse an enemy.

Aerial view of the hill fort, clearly showing the development of the earthworks and entrances

I mile N of Oswestry, off unclassified road off A483
OS Map 126, ref SJ 295310

History

The romantically named 'white ladies' of this priory were medieval nuns – Augustinian canonesses, who, as their name suggests, wore habits of undyed cloth. Most of the major religious orders founded convents for women, who followed a similar rule to that of their male counterparts. The first reference to the Priory of St Leonard, now known as White Ladies Priory, is a grant of land dated 1186; the architectural evidence also suggests a late 12th-century foundation date.

Unusually for a monastic site, the buildings seem to have been little altered throughout their 350-year history. White Ladies was never a large or rich house, and in 1535 there were just six nuns left, with an annual income of £17. The following year, it was one of the first religious houses to be suppressed, though four nuns apparently remained until 1538.

After the suppression of the monasteries most of the convent buildings were taken down, though parts of the church remained. The site

White Ladies Priory from the south-east

passed through various owners, notably the Skevington family. They built a large timber-framed house here, though this was demolished in the 18th century. A brief moment of high drama came in 1651 when, following his defeat at the Battle of Worcester, the future Charles II hid here, disguised as a woodsman with his face darkened with soot. By then, both the priory and nearby Boscobel House (see p. 101) were owned by the Giffords, a Roman Catholic family, and the church precinct was used for Catholic burials until 1844.

Description

The nuns' church was a relatively small and plain building without aisles. Several walls survive to their original height. At the east end is the presbytery, now just a low wall, where the high altar stood. The nuns' choir stalls stood to the west of this between two small transepts. The wide, round-headed archway leads from the choir into the foundations of the north transept. As elsewhere in the church,

One of the finely carved capitals on the north wall

the arch, column shafts and capitals are skilfully carved in a solid, simple design typical of the best Romanesque architecture.

The west end of the church has no door but there are remains of two windows. Doorways lead out of the nave to the north and south. The north door led into the cloister, now a mere platform on the ground. This was probably timber-framed, hence the lack of standing remains. The plan of White Ladies was unusual in having the cloister and domestic buildings on the north side of the church rather than on the south. The fairly low roof line of the church perhaps ensured that these buildings were not always in shade, and their position may have been chosen because it was nearer to the water supply. The wall on the south side enclosed the burial ground. Hard against the east wall was the Tudor timber-framed house built by the Skevington family.

1 mile SW of Boscobel House, off unclassified road between A41 and A5
OS Map 127, ref SJ 826076
Open
1 Apr–31 Oct:
10am–5pm daily;
closed 1 Nov–
31 Mar

The south transept and chapter house of Croxden Abbey

History

Croxden Abbey was founded in 1176 with lands and money given by Bertram de Verdun, lord of nearby Alton Castle. The founder monks came from the abbey of Aunay-sur-Odon in Normandy, which belonged to the reforming Cistercian order. The Cistercians followed an austere life of prayer and manual labour, and sought to be self-sufficient, farming the surrounding land.

After initially settling at Cotton, the monks moved three years later to nearby Croxden, where work began immediately on the construction of the church, followed by the buildings around the cloister. Further enlargement followed under the prosperous leadership of Walter London, abbot 1242–68.

Croxden was never a wealthy abbey. It flourished during the 13th century when it may have supported as many as 70 monks. During the 14th century the community suffered from the effects of crop failure, cattle disease and plague, although despite such setbacks an impressive new house was built for the abbot in 1335. The abbey was eventually suppressed by Henry VIII in 1538, and the site became part of a farm.

Description

The abbey site is now bisected by a road cutting diagonally through the church. The east end of the church lies on one side, while the nave, south transept and most of the other monastic buildings are on the other. Some walls survive to a height of 18m

(60ft) or more and are finely detailed; others are mere foundations or are hidden under the adjacent farmhouse and other buildings. The site covered almost 30ha (74 acres) and was originally enclosed by perimeter walls, some of which survive.

The church is a fine example of Cistercian architecture, at once austere and imposing. Its most remarkable feature is the east end, which was rebuilt from the 1190s in a most unusual form. The foundations show that it was semicircular, and surrounded by an aisle and five projecting chapels; English Cistercian churches usually had plain, rectangular east ends.

The square cloister, south of the road, was the centre of monastic life: a place for the monks to work and read and containing a covered walkway connecting the principal buildings. The western range of the cloister – now partly beneath the farmhouse – probably accommodated the lay brothers who performed most of the abbey's manual work. In the

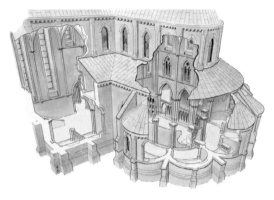

A reconstruction of the east end of the church, as rebuilt from the 1190s onwards

south range – where only the south wall survives – stood the refectory, kitchens and warming room. In the well-preserved east range were the chapter house for daily meetings, the parlour, day room and sacristy; the monks' dormitory occupied the floor above. At the south end, the stone-lined drain of the latrines is still visible. A passage led through this range to the monks' infirmary, where old, sick and convalescing monks could be cared for; three pairs of stone table rests survive in what was the dining hall. To the south is the abbot's lodging of 1335.

5 miles NW
of Uttoxeter
off A5030
OS Map 128,
ref SK 066397
Open
10am–5pm daily

87

During the late 18th century, at a time of great social and economic change, many literary, scientific and philosophical societies were formed, bringing together like-minded people, mainly men, for dining and discussion. Important among these was the Lunar Society, founded in Birmingham in 1765. Its name was an allusion to the fact that the society met once a month on the Monday nearest to the full moon, when the extra light made the journey home through unlit streets easier.

The society included many famous and influential scientists, industrialists, inventors, entrepreneurs and theorists among its members. At its centre were five men of different professions and backgrounds: the metalwork manufacturer Matthew Boulton; the engineer James Watt; the potter Josiah Wedgwood; Erasmus Darwin, philosopher, medical practitioner, poet and grandfather of Charles Darwin (as was Wedgwood); and the chemist and radical preacher Joseph Priestley. The group met mostly at Boulton's home, Soho House, Birmingham. Others frequently present included the chemist James Keir, William Murdoch, Boulton's personal physician William Small and William Withering. Among leading international scientists who corresponded with the group were the Frenchman Antoine Lavoisier and the American Benjamin Franklin.

The members of the Lunar Society came together to pursue their enthusiasms for technology, scientific and engineering inventions, natural philosophy and medicine, and these topics naturally formed the focus of their meetings. They played an important role in furthering industrial and technological change in England through collaborative inventions and experiments, which Erasmus

An engraving by Deschamps showing a meeting of the Lunar Society in the 1780s

Darwin described as 'a little philosophical laughing'. At least 10 members were eventually elected Fellows of the Royal Society. Darwin, for example, besides practising medicine, devised a new design for canal lifts and invented a device for grinding pigments that Wedgwood employed at his ceramics factory, Etruria, in Staffordshire. Wedgwood and Boulton worked together to produce ceramic cameo jewellery set in cut-steel mounts, and Wedgwood also supplied other members of the society with chemicals for their scientific experiments. Many members – including Watt – produced designs for steam engines, and were keen to explore their wider applications. The society was a strong supporter of applied research that had practical outcomes. In 1793, for example, Dr Thomas Beddoes proposed a medical institute where newly discovered gases could be tested to investigate whether they could cure diseases such as consumption.

Not all the society's experiments had a exclusively serious purpose: in 1784, Darwin made his first attempt to send a 'balloon post' from Derby to his fellow Lunar men in Birmingham, only to learn

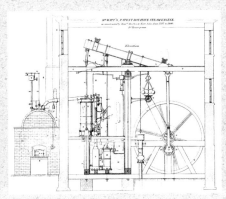

Drawing (1787) of a steam engine manufactured by Boulton and Watt in Soho, Birmingham

that 'the wicked wind' had carried it off course. Boulton also attempted to find out by using a firework attached to a balloon whether 'the growling of thunder is owing to echoes, or to successive explosions'.

The society enjoyed its most active period in the 1780s, but towards the end of the century it fell into decline and was officially closed in 1813. Many of its original members had died by the 1820s. Nevertheless, the group had a lasting influence on developments in science, industry and the arts; above all, they were optimistic about the progress of the human race.

The north barn of Halesowen Abbey, incorporating medieval masonry and timbers

History

In 1214, King John gave the manor of Hales, Shropshire, to Peter des Roches, Bishop of Winchester, to build there a religious house of 'whatever order he pleased'. The abbey at Halesowen was established four years later. Dedicated to the Virgin and St John the Evangelist, it was colonised by canons from the existing Premonstratensian monastery at Welbeck, Nottinghamshire. The Premonstratensians were not monks in the strict sense but rather communities of priests living together under the rule of the order. The order followed that of the Cistercians, valuing an austere and secluded life. They became known as the 'white canons' as they dressed in undyed habits.

For more than 300 years the monks controlled a vast estate around Halesowen, although an uprising by local people against the abbot is recorded after he forced them to pay a series of punitive taxes. The monastery acted as a resting point for pilgrims to nearby St Kenelm's Church, Romsley, said to have been built near the site where Kenelm, King of Mercia, had been martyred. The waters of St Kenelm's spring there were thought to have healing properties.

The abbey and all its possessions were surrendered to the Crown by its last abbot, William Taylor, in 1538, and two years later the monastic buildings were partly demolished. Henry VIII granted the abbey estate to Sir John Dudley, who passed it to his servant George Tuckey. Parts of the monastic buildings were later incorporated into the north barn of Manor Farm. The abbey came into the guardianship of the state in 1915.

Description

The main abbey buildings lie among the 19th-century agricultural buildings and farmhouse of Manor Farm (not in the care of English Heritage). They were originally situated within a rectangular precinct, defined by man-made fishponds to the north, south and south-west and by water-filled ditches. The monastic church was built of local red sandstone, and its standing remains – including parts of the presbytery, south transept, east end and south aisle – are thought to date from the early 13th century. A range of agricultural buildings overlies the south wall of the church and north part of the cloister. The north barn, probably dating from the 17th century, follows the same alignment as the church and has been partly built from reused medieval masonry and timbers. Excavations at the site during the late 19th and early 20th centuries confirmed that the barn incorporates standing fragments of the monastic church. Of the south range of the cloister, the south wall of the refectory and its undercroft remain standing. To the south-east of the church is a two-storeyed building constructed in the second half of the 13th century, which may have been the abbot's lodging.

Engraving of Halesowen Abbey by Samuel and Nathaniel Buck, 1731

Off A456
Kidderminster
road, ½ mile W
of M5 Junction 3
OS Map 139,
ref SP 975828
Contact regional
office for opening
times and access
Tel: 0121 625 6820

91

LEIGH COURT BARN

History

This barn is the only surviving building from the manor of Leigh Court, which belonged in the Middle Ages to the monks of Pershore. There were once other farm buildings and houses, and the abbot himself is known to have sometimes resided here. Medieval monasteries owned farmland that could supply them with food and raw materials, either directly, or indirectly through the sale of surplus produce. Monastic farms, known as granges, were often large-scale operations, and the size and magnificence of the grange barn at Leigh Court suggests that the Pershore Abbey farm was a well-organised and lucrative business. Radiocarbon dating supports the evidence of carpentry techniques that date the barn to the 14th century, probably about 1325. With the closure of the abbey in 1540 the farm passed into lay hands. Until relatively recently the need for large barns for storing and threshing grain remained unchanged. Thanks, no doubt, to its size and sturdy construction, the barn has survived largely unaltered for almost 700 years.

Description

The barn measures over 43m (141ft) long, 11m (36ft) wide and 9m (29ft 6in) high. Characteristically, barns had pairs of doors on opposite sides, with the threshing floor between them; the floor here is made of flagstones. With the doors open, the

Leigh Court Barn, one of the earliest surviving cruck barns in Britain

wind blew through the building to winnow the grain, which was tossed in the breeze until all the dust and chaff blew away. Externally the barn is part-weatherboarded, though the steep angle of the tiled roof suggests that it may once have been thatched.

Inside, the most distinctive features are the massive crucks – nine pairs of curved timbers like huge ribs that support the main structure. Cruck construction was adopted early in the 14th century, and this is the largest and one of the oldest surviving cruck barns in Britain. The shape of each cruck is determined by the oak tree from which it was sawn. The crucks do not directly support the ridge at the top. Instead, this rests on yokes and posts that compensate for the different cruck lengths. Rather than being carried by the outer walls, the main weight of the roof is transmitted to the base wall via the crucks. Laterally, the crucks are tied together by collar beams, in turn strengthened by arched braces. The timbers are fixed with wooden pegs, not nails or

Detail of the barn's roof construction

screws. A few timbers were replaced during repair in 1987–8.

The outer walls of the barn were originally filled with tall single panels of wattle and daub, or wooden rods interwoven with twigs or branches and covered with mud or clay. Over the centuries, these have mostly been replaced with brick infilling. The barn's timber frame rests on a plinth of red sandstone blocks, now largely encased in brick. Unfortunately, inadequate foundations caused the walls to splay out, a problem remedied by underpinning during restoration.

5 miles W of Worcester on unclassified road off A4103
OS Map 150, ref 783535
Open
1 Apr–30 Sep: 10am–6pm Thurs–Sun and Bank Hol Mons

Twelve English Heritage sites in the East Midlands and eleven in the West Midlands are staffed. Most have a separate guidebook, which can be bought at the site's gift shop or through mail order. These sites charge an admission fee, although admission is free to members of English Heritage (see inside back cover). Please note that sites listed here as opening 1 April open for Easter if it is earlier. Full details of admission charges, access and opening times for all English Heritage sites are given in the *English Heritage Members' and Visitors' Handbook*, and on our website (www.english-heritage.org.uk).

Details of English Heritage publications can be found in the *Publishing Catalogue*. To obtain a free copy of the catalogue, and to order English Heritage publications, please contact:

English Heritage Postal Sales,
c/o Gillards, Trident Works,
Temple Cloud, Bristol BS39 5AZ
Tel: 01761 452966 Fax: 01761 453408
E-mail: ehsales@gillards.com

ASHBY DE LA ZOUCH CASTLE

LEICESTERSHIRE

Ashby de la Zouch Castle forms the backdrop to the famous jousting scenes in Sir Walter Scott's classic novel *Ivanhoe*. The earliest remains appear to date to the mid-12th century. Between 1474 and 1483, William, Lord Hastings, Lord Chamberlain to Edward IV, constructed the tower that bears his name.

Open year-round. Please call for admission prices and opening times: 01530 413343.

In Ashby de la Zouch, 12 miles S of Derby on A511. Restricted parking on site; please park in the town car park.
OS Map 128, ref SK 361166.

BOLSOVER CASTLE

Bolsover Castle stands on the site of a medieval castle built by the Peveril family shortly after the Norman Conquest. It was later bought by Sir Charles Cavendish, who began work on the Little Castle – a building for leisure and lavish entertaining – in 1612. His son, William, inherited the Little Castle in 1616 and set about its completion. He also added the Terrace Range and the impressive Riding House.

Open year-round. Please call for admission prices and opening times: 01246 822844.

In Bolsover, 6 miles E of Chesterfield on A632. Off M1 at junctions 29 or 30, 6 miles from Mansfield. *OS Map 120, ref SK 470707.*

GAINSBOROUGH OLD HALL
LINCOLNSHIRE

Gainsborough Old Hall, over 500 years old, has a medieval kitchen, a great hall and Tudor brick tower. John Wesley preached three times in the great hall here in the 18th century.

Open year-round. Please call for admission prices and opening times: 01427 612669. Managed by Lincolnshire County Council.

In Gainsborough, opposite the library. *OS Map 112, ref SK 813900.*

HARDWICK OLD HALL
DERBYSHIRE

This large, ruined house was the family home of Bess of Hardwick, one of the most remarkable women of the Elizabethan age. She rebuilt the house in a grand and lavish style in the 1580s and 1590s, before embarking on the magnificent New Hall nearby.

Open 1 Apr–31 Oct. Please call for admission prices and opening times: 01246 850431. Owned by the National Trust and managed by English Heritage.

9 1/2 miles SE of Chesterfield, off A6175, from junction 29 of M1.
OS Map 120, ref SK 462637.

KIRBY HALL
NORTHAMPTONSHIRE

Kirby Hall is one of the great Elizabethan houses. The great hall and state rooms remain intact and have recently been refitted and redecorated to authentic 17th- and 18th-century designs. The fine late 17th-century gardens have been partly restored and are laid out in an elaborate 'cutwork' pattern.

Open year-round. Please call for admission prices and opening times: 01536 203230. Owned by the Earl of Winchilsea and managed by English Heritage.

On unclassified road off A43, 4 miles NE of Corby.
OS Map 141, ref SP 926927.

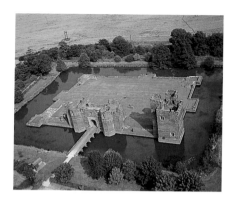

KIRBY MUXLOE CASTLE

LEICESTERSHIRE

This picturesque moated brick castle was begun in 1480 by William, Lord Hastings, a prominent supporter of Edward IV who also owned Ashby de la Zouch Castle (see p. 94). After the king's death in 1483, however, he was denounced as a traitor and beheaded. The castle was left unfinished, and only the west tower and part of the gatehouse were built.

Open Please call for admission prices and opening times: 01162 386886.

4 miles W of Leicester, off B5380; close to M1 junction 21A, northbound exit only.
OS Map 140, ref SK 524046.

LINCOLN MEDIEVAL BISHOPS' PALACE

LINCOLNSHIRE

Constructed in the late 12th century, the medieval bishops' palace at Lincoln was once one of the most important buildings in England. As the administrative centre of the largest diocese in the country, its architecture reflected the enormous power and wealth of the bishops as princes of the church. Built on hillside terraces, the palace has views of the cathedral and the Roman, medieval and modern city.

Open year-round. Please call for admission prices and opening times: 01522 527468.

On the S side of Lincoln Cathedral.
OS Map 121, ref SK 978717.

LYDDINGTON BEDE HOUSE

Lyddington Bede House was originally one wing of a medieval palace of the Bishops of Lincoln. In 1600, the buildings were converted into almshouses, and they served as homes for pensioners for over 300 years.

Open 1 Apr–31 Oct. Please call for admission prices and opening times: 01572 822438.

In Lyddington, 6 miles N of Corby; 1 mile E of A6003, next to the church
OS Map 141, ref SP 876970.

PEVERIL CASTLE

Known as the 'Castle of the Peak' during the Middle Ages, Peveril Castle is perched high above the village of Castleton, and offers breathtaking views of the Peak District. Founded in the 11th century by one of William the Conqueror's knights, William Peverel, the castle provided a defensible stronghold and residence for several centuries.

Open year-round. Please call for admission prices and opening times: 01433 620613.

Via the market place in Castleton; 15 miles W of Sheffield on A6187.
OS Map 110, ref SK 149826.

RUSHTON TRIANGULAR LODGE

This extraordinary triangular building was designed and built by Sir Thomas Tresham, an Elizabethan landowner, between 1593 and 1597. The Lodge is a testament to Tresham's Roman Catholicism: the number three, symbolising the Holy Trinity, is apparent everywhere. There are three floors and three walls, trefoil windows and three triangular gables on each side.

Open 1 Apr–31 Oct. Please call for admission prices and opening times: 01536 710761.

1 mile W of Rushton, on unclassified road; 3 miles from Desborough on A6.
OS Map 141, ref SP 830831.

SIBSEY TRADER WINDMILL

LINCOLNSHIRE

This traditional working windmill, towering over the flat Lincolnshire landscape, was built in 1877. Its six-storey tower contains original working machinery, and the mill still produces a range of flours from organically grown grain.

Open year-round. Please call for admission prices and opening times: 01205 750036. Managed by Ian Ansell.

½ mile W of Sibsey, off A16 5 miles N of Boston. *OS Map 122, ref TF 345511.*

WINGFIELD MANOR

DERBYSHIRE

Now a huge ruin, Wingfield Manor was built in 1440 by Ralph, Lord Cromwell, Treasurer of England. In the 16th century, Mary, Queen of Scots, was imprisoned here several times. Though the manor has been unoccupied since the 1770s, the late Gothic great hall and the high tower are testaments to its heyday.

Open year-round. Please call for admission prices and opening times: 01773 832060.

Wingfield Manor is contained within a private working farm and partly surrounds the farmhouse. Visitors are asked to respect the privacy of the owners and keep to the official routes. No visits outside official opening hours.

11 miles S of Chesterfield on B5035; ½ mile S of South Wingfield.
OS Map 119, ref SK 374548.

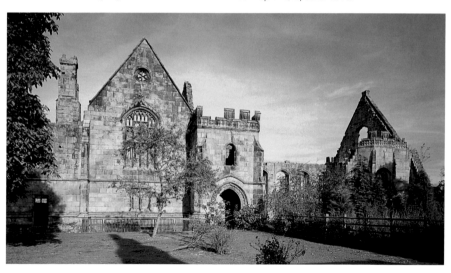

BOSCOBEL HOUSE AND THE ROYAL OAK

SHROPSHIRE

Boscobel House was built in about 1632, when John Gifford of Whiteladies converted a timber-framed farmhouse into a hunting lodge. Following his defeat at the Battle of Worcester in 1651, the future King Charles II sought refuge at Boscobel. He hid first in the tree now known as the Royal Oak and then spent the night in a priest-hole in the attic. He was escorted to a safe house before escaping to France.

Open 1 Apr–31 Oct. Please call for admission prices and opening times: 01902 850244.

On minor road from A41 to A5, 8 miles NW of Wolverhampton. 5 minute drive from junction 3 of M54.
OS Map 127, ref SJ 837083.

BUILDWAS ABBEY
SHROPSHIRE

Set beside the River Severn, against a backdrop of wooded grounds a short distance from the Iron Bridge, are the extensive remains of this Cistercian abbey founded in 1135.

Open 1 Apr–30 Sep. Please call for admission prices and opening times: 01952 433274.

On S bank of River Severn on A4169, 2 miles W of Ironbridge.

OS Map 127, ref SJ 643043.

GOODRICH CASTLE
HEREFORDSHIRE

This fortress stands majestically on a crag commanding the passage of the River Wye into the picturesque wooded valley at Symonds Yat. Its medieval buildings, including the Norman tower, are still largely intact, and are protected by wide and deep ditches cut into the rock.

Open year-round. Please call for admission prices and opening times: 01600 890538.

5 miles S of Ross-on-Wye off A40.
OS Map 162, ref SO 577200.

KENILWORTH CASTLE
WARWICKSHIRE

Kenilworth has been linked with some of the most important names in English history. Here, Elizabeth I was entertained by the Earl of Leicester. Today, with its impressive Norman keep, medieval great hall, and restored Elizabethan gardens and Leicester's Tower, it is among the largest historic sites in England.

Open year-round. Please call for admission prices and opening times: 01926 852078.

In Kenilworth.
OS Map 140, ref SP 278723.

HAUGHMOND ABBEY
SHROPSHIRE

The extensive remains of this 12th-century Augustinian abbey comprise one of the best-surviving medieval monastic sites in Shropshire. Until its suppression in the 1530s, it played an active and important role in the economic and political life of the region.

Open 1 Apr–30 Sep. Please call for admission prices and opening times: 01743 709661.

3 miles NE of Shrewsbury off B5062.
OS Map 126, ref SJ 542152.

MORTIMER'S CROSS WATER MILL
HEREFORDSHIRE

This 18th-century water mill remains partly in working order. There are attractive gardens, woodland walks and a stone weir nearby, as well as an important limestone quarry.

Open Easter–Sep, Sat and Sun 10am–4pm; other times by arrangement. Please call for admission prices and further information: 01568 708820.

7 miles NW of Leominster on B4362.
OS Map 148, ref SO 426637.

STOKESAY CASTLE
SHROPSHIRE

Situated on the Welsh borders, Stokesay Castle has survived remarkably intact since the late 13th century, when it was built by Lawrence of Ludlow, a leading wool merchant. The manor house that he constructed was both an impressive fortification and a comfortable residence, designed as a statement of wealth and power.

Open year-round. Please call for admission prices and opening times: 01588 672544.

7 miles NW of Ludlow off A49.
OS Map 148, ref SO 446787.

WALL ROMAN SITE (LETOCETUM)
STAFFORDSHIRE

Wall was an important staging post on Watling Street, the Roman military road to north Wales. It provided overnight accommodation for travelling Roman officials and imperial messengers. The foundations of an inn and bathhouse can be seen, and many of the excavated finds are displayed in the on-site museum.

Open 1 Apr–31 Oct. Please call for admission prices and opening times: 01543 480768. Owned by the National Trust and managed by English Heritage.

Off A5 at Wall, near Lichfield.
OS Map 139, ref SK 098066.

WENLOCK PRIORY
SHROPSHIRE

A religious house was founded here in the late seventh century, when its abbess, St Milburge, became famous for the miracles she was said to have performed. The ruins of the Cluniac priory that replaced it in the 11th century include one of the largest monastic churches in the country.

Open year-round. Please call for admission prices and opening times: 01952 727466.

In Much Wenlock.
OS Map 127, ref SJ 625001.

WITLEY COURT
WORCESTERSHIRE

Witley Court was remodelled in the 19th century into a vast mansion, first by John Nash and later in the Italianate style by Samuel Daukes. The spectacular ruins of this once great house are surrounded by magnificent landscaped gardens designed by William Nesfield and containing elaborate fountains.

Open year-round. Please call for admission prices and opening times: 01299 896636.

10 miles NW of Worcester on A443.
OS Map 150, ref SO 769649.

WROXETER ROMAN CITY
SHROPSHIRE

Wroxeter was the fourth largest city in Roman Britain. Originally a legionary fortress, it later developed into a thriving civilian city populated by retired soldiers and traders. Today, the most impressive features are the second-century municipal baths and the remains of the huge wall dividing them from the exercise hall, right in the city's heart.

Open year-round. Please call for admission prices and opening times: 01743 761330.

At Wroxeter, 5 miles E of Shrewsbury on B4380.
OS Map 126, ref SJ 565087.

INDEX

INDEX

FURTHER READING

EAST MIDLANDS
DERBYSHIRE

Arbor Low Henge and Stone Circle and Gib Hill Barrow, Hob Hurst's House and Nine Ladies Stone Circle

Barnatt, J and Smith, K *The Peak District: Landscapes through Time*. Macclesfield: Windgather Press, 2004

Edmonds, M and Seaborne, T *Prehistory in the Peak*. Stroud: Tempus Publishing, 2001

Sutton Scarsdale Hall

Gomme, A 'The Genesis of Sutton Scarsdale'. *Architectural History*, vol. 24, 1981, pp. 34–8

Worsley, L 'Sutton Scarsdale'. *SPAB News*, vol. 22, no. 4, 2001, pp. 26–9

LEICESTERSHIRE

Jewry Wall, Leicester

Jarvis, P 'The Early Pits of the Jewry Wall Site, Leicester'. *Leicestershire Archaeological and Historical Society Transactions*, vol. 60, 1986, pp. 7–15

Rutland, R A *The Jewry Wall*. Leicester: Leicestershire Museums, Art Galleries and Records Service, 1976

LINCOLNSHIRE

Bolingbroke Castle

Drewett, P L and Freke, D J 'The Great Hall at Bolingbroke Castle, Lincolnshire'. *Medieval Archaeology*, vol. 18, 1974, pp. 163–5

Thompson, M W 'The Origins of Bolingbroke Castle, Lincolnshire'. *Medieval Archaeology*, vol. 10, 1966, pp. 152–8

Thompson, M W 'Further Work at Bolingbroke Castle, Lincolnshire'. *Medieval Archaeology*, vol. 13, 1969, pp. 216–17

Tattershall College

Douglas Simpson, W (ed.) *The Building Accounts of Tattershall Castle 1434–1472*. Lincoln Record Society, vol. 55, 1960

NORTHAMPTONSHIRE

Chichele College

Charlton, J 'The Chichele College, Higham Ferrers'. *Archaeological Journal*, vol. 110, 1953, p. 193

Pevsner, N and Cherry, B *The Buildings of England: Northamptonshire*. New Haven/London: Yale University Press, 2nd edn, 1973

Eleanor Cross, Geddington

Powrie, J *Eleanor of Castile*. Studley: Brewin Books, 1990

Priestland, P and Priestland, M *In Memory of Eleanor: the Story of the Eleanor Crosses*. Nottingham: Ashbracken, 1990

NOTTINGHAMSHIRE

Mattersey Priory

Charlton, J *Mattersey Priory, Nottinghamshire*. London: HMSO, 1972

Rufford Abbey

McGee, C and Perkins, J 'A Study of the Cisterican Abbey at Rufford, Nottinghamshire', in Alexander, J S (ed.) *Southwell and Nottinghamshire: Medieval Art, Architecture and Industry*, British Archaeological Association Conference Transactions, 21. Leeds: British Archaeological Association, 1998, pp. 83–92

Phillips, A P 'The Diet of the Savile Household in the 17th Century'. *Transactions of the Thoroton Society of Nottinghamshire*, vol. 93, 1960, pp. 57–71

Rufford Abbey: Glimpses of the Past. Nottingham: Nottinghamshire County Council Leisure Services, 1994

FURTHER READING

WEST MIDLANDS

HEREFORDSHIRE

Arthur's Stone

Children, G and Nash, G *A Guide to Prehistoric Sites in Herefordshire.* Woonton Almeley: Logaston Press, 1994

Gibson, A and Simpson, D (eds.) *Prehistoric Ritual and Religion: Essays in Honour of Aubrey Burl.* Stroud: Sutton Publishing, 1998

Edvin Loach Old Church

Merlen, R H A *The Motte-and-Bailey Castles of the Welsh Border.* Ludlow: Palmers Press, 1987

Salter, M *Old Parish Churches of Herefordshire.* Malvern: Folly Publications, 1998

Longtown Castle

Merlen, R H A *The Motte-and-Bailey Castles of the Welsh Border.* Ludlow: Palmers Press, 1987

Remfry, P M *Longtown Castle 1048 to 1241.* Malvern Link: SCS Publishing, 2003

Salter, M *The Castles of Herefordshire and Worcestershire.* Malvern: Folly Publications, 2000

Rotherwas Chapel

Fisher, M *Pugin-land: A W N Pugin, Lord Shrewsbury and the Gothic Revival in Staffordshire.* Stafford: Michael Fisher Publ., 2002

Wigmore Castle

Channer, J 'Wigmore Castle'. *SPAB News*, vol. 22, no. 4, 2001, pp. 21–5

Remfry, P M *The Mortimers of Wigmore, Part 1: Wigmore Castle 1066–1181.* Malvern Link: SCS Publishing, 1995

Remfry, P M *Wigmore Castle Tourist Guide.* Malvern Link: SCS Publishing, 2000

SHROPSHIRE

Acton Burnell Castle

Ascott-Symms, J *Castles of Shropshire.* Artscape Books, 1989

Jackson, M *Castles of Shropshire.* Shrewsbury: Shropshire Libraries, 1988

Ralegh Radford, C A *Acton Burnell Castle, Shropshire.* London: HMSO, 1957

Salter, M *Castles and Moated Mansions of Shropshire.* Malvern: Folly Publishers, 2001

West, J 'Acton Burnell Castle, a Re-interpretation', in Detsias, A (ed.) *Collectanea Historica.* Maidstone, 1981, pp. 85–92

Cantlop Bridge

Blackwall, A *Historic Bridges of Shropshire.* Shrewsbury: Shropshire Libraries, 1985

Burton, A *Thomas Telford.* London: Aurum Press, 1999

Sutherland, R J M *Structural Iron, 1750–1850.* Aldershot: Ashgate, 1997

Clun Castle

'Clun Castle', in Munby, J and Summerson, H *Stokesay Castle.* London: English Heritage, 2002

Renn, D F *Norman Castles in Britain.* London: John Baker, 1968

Iron Bridge

Clark, C M *The English Heritage Book of Ironbridge Gorge.* London: Batsford/English Heritage, 1993

Cossons, N and Trinder, B *The Iron Bridge: Symbol of the Industrial Revolution.* Chichester: Phillimore, rev. edn, 2002

Langley Chapel

Garner, L *Churches of Shropshire.* Shrewsbury: Shropshire Books, 1994

Morriss, R 'Langley Chapel, Shropshire – A Brief Guide'. Unpublished typescript, Shrewsbury Records and Research Library

FURTHER READING

Randall, G *Church Furnishings and Decoration in England and Wales*. London: Batsford, 1980

Lilleshall Abbey

Ferris, I *Haughmond Abbey, Lilleshall Abbey and Moreton Corbet Castle*. London: English Heritage, 2000

Rigold, S E *Lilleshall Abbey*. London: English Heritage, 1989

Mitchell's Fold Stone Circle

Burl, A *The Stone Circles of Britain, Ireland and Brittany*. New Haven/London: Yale University Press, 2000

Dickens, G *Shropshire Seasons*. Shrewsbury: Shropshire Books, 1993

Grinsell, L *Mitchell's Fold Stone Circle and its Folklore*. St Peter Port: Toucan Press, 1980

Moreton Corbet Castle

Ferris, I *Haughmond Abbey, Lilleshall Abbey and Moreton Corbet Castle*. London: English Heritage, 2000

Pevsner, N *The Buildings of England: Shropshire*. London: Penguin, 1958

Weaver, O J 'Moreton Corbet Castle'. *Archaeological Journal*, vol. 138, 1981, p. 44

Old Oswestry Hill Fort

Hughes, G 'Old Oswestry Hillfort: Excavations by W J Varley 1939–40'. *Archaeologia Cambrensis*, vol. 143, 1994, pp. 46–91

Martin, P 'The Historical Ecology of Old Oswestry'. *Shropshire Botanical Society*, autumn 1999, pp. 11–12

White Ladies Priory

Gilyard-Beer, R *White Ladies Priory*. London: HMSO, 1982

Northcote, P *A Twelfth Century Nun*. Oxford: Oxford University Press, 1966

Weaver, O J *Boscobel House and White Ladies Priory*. London: English Heritage, 1987

STAFFORDSHIRE

Croxden Abbey

Baillie Reynolds, P *Croxden Abbey, Staffordshire*. London: HMSO, 1946, rev. edn 1969

WEST MIDLANDS

Halesowen Abbey

Molyneux, N A D 'A Late Thirteenth-Century Building at Halesowen'. *Transactions of the Worcestershire Archaeological Society*, series 3, vol. 9, 1984, pp. 45–53

WORCESTERSHIRE

Leigh Court Barn

Charles, F W B and Horn, H 'The Cruck-built Barn of Leigh Court, Worcestershire, England'. *Journal of the Society of Architectural Historians*, vol. 32, 1973, pp. 5–29

Griswold, J *Medieval English Tithe Barn*s. Lebanon, NH: New England University Press, 1999

Spence, K 'A Barn to Boast About'. *Country Life*, vol. 181, 26 March 1987, p. 198

FURTHER READING AND WEBSITES

FEATURES

Creswell Crags: Ice Age Cave Art

www.creswell-crags.org.uk

The Derwent Valley Mills World Heritage Site

The Derwent Valley Mills and their Communities.
Derby: Derwent Valley Mills Partnership, 2001
(comprehensive guide to the World Heritage
site based on the nomination for inscription on the World
Heritage list in 2001)

**The Boot and Shoe Industry of
Northamptonshire**

Morrison, K A and Bond, A *Built to Last? The
Buildings of the Northamptonshire Boot and Shoe
Industry.* London: English Heritage, 2004

**Wigmore Castle: A New Approach to
Conservation**

Coppack, G 'Conserved in the Gentle Hands
of Nature', www.ihbc.org.uk/context_archive/73/
nature_dir/nature_s.htm

Palmer, M 'Romancing the Stone'. *Heritage Today*,
48, December 1999, pp. 12–16

'Archaeological Activities Undertaken by English
Heritage: Midlands', in Olivier, A C H (ed.)
Archaeological Review 1995–6, 1996, pp. 51–2

Thomas Telford: 'The Colossus of Roads'

Burton, A *Thomas Telford.* London: Aurum Press,
2000

**'Reaching for the Moon': The Lunar Society
of Birmingham**

Uglow, J *The Lunar Men.* London: Faber and Faber,
2003

Useful websites relating to the Midlands:

GENERAL

www.english-heritage.org.uk
(English Heritage)

www.nationaltrust.org.uk
(National Trust)

EAST MIDLANDS

www.peakdistrict.org
(Peak District National Park Authority)

www.lincsheritage.org
(Heritage Lincolnshire)

www.east-northamptonshire.gov.uk
(East Northamptonshire Council)

www.lincolnshire.gov.uk
(Lincolnshire County Council)

www.nottscc.gov.uk
(Nottinghamshire County Council)

WEST MIDLANDS

www.visitheartofengland.com
(Visit Heart of England website)

www.herefordshire.gov.uk
(Herefordshire County Council)

www.shropshire.gov.uk
(Shropshire County Council)

www.staffordshire.gov.uk
(Staffordshire County Council)

www.worcestershire.gov.uk
(Worcestershire County Council)